Read the covers? You wa

There's a book *before this one* that majors on cricket and Mad Ideas. This one is marginally more growed-up but still bristles from within the Football, Cricket *& Everything* family, making it both something of a sequel, to 'The Dots Will Not Be Joined', and unique. (Again).

'Beautiful Games' will do what it says on the tin: draw you in to a life in movement/family/sport/travel/teams/learning and sport. It will dip your head into tragedy and prejudice, as well as into godlike bliss. There will be cannonballs; there will be knives; there will be Italians. Later there will be enquiries into what the hell we have to do, to get fit and well.

There are three sections. 'Formations' starts in a mire of weird-but-all-pervasive discrimination and soon leads us to grief. Fun-fact: I nearly called this book 'Heading' because of... well, you'll see. This section unashamedly hurls itself between Big Relatable Stories. I hope it asks similarly monumental questions about the roles of homage and influence and family culture: it does find plenty joy!

'Practice' is more about an *actual life in games*... and who has inspired that... and has some fun with how. So brilliance and yeh – good practice. 'The Case for Sport' digs in to research and to meanings around Sport Development. And campaigns, just a little.

A good lump of this is autobiographical; not, I hope out of arrogance but to be clear and true vis-à-vis *accuracy* and my right to comment. I was born into an active mob. I still *do play*. I *am* a coach, teacher and writer. In a former life (as a young playwright) some intellectual geezer called me a 'free-wheeling absurdist'.

Happy days. I'm still rollin'.

Love to all, Rick.

Front cover pic: my three bros in the garden at 43 Oak Road. About 1967. Great boots!

...Also by Rick Walton.

THE DOTS WILL NOT BE JOINED: Football. Cricket. *Stories*.

Available from your on-line behemoth. Possibly a prequel to the book you have in your hand.

(Possibly) an e-book of selected posts, called UNWEIGHTED – the bowlingatvincent compendium... which may or may not still be available.

Hundreds of free blogs at bowlingatvincent.com and sportslaureate.co.uk – formerly cricketmanwales.com

(At time of writing) two Twitter/X accounts: @sportslaureate and @bowlingatvinny. The former mainly does what you'd think, the latter is spikier, artsier and 'more political'.

The bowlingatvincent multinational
corporation brings you

BEAUTIFUL GAMES.

BY
RICK WALTON

Grosvenor House
Publishing Limited

The right of Rick Walton to be identified as the author of this
work has been asserted in accordance with Section 78
of the Copyright, Designs and Patents Act 1988

The book cover is copyright to Rick Walton

This book is published by
Grosvenor House Publishing Ltd
Link House
140 The Broadway, Tolworth, Surrey, KT6 7HT.
www.grosvenorhousepublishing.co.uk

A CIP record for this book
is available from the British Library

ISBN 978-1-80381-776-7

Possibly-questionable quotation; on the grounds that it's superfluous, at-best only distantly-relevant to what follows... and therefore pretentious, dwaarlinks:

Everywhere we look we find "binaries where thinking once existed".

Naomi Klein.

CONTENTS

DEDICATION.

To family, friends and brilliant, brilliant colleagues.

*And with a hearty hug, to Cliff Winship
and Linda Hay – née Dye:*

RIP, from '23.

All Town, aren't we?

THE PROLOGUE.

Always been happy enough to place the target on my own back. Always been conscious that things that are too comfortable perpetuate, well – everything. Would rather be misunderstood than mollify the Meaning of Things… so here we go again.

*It's gonna date me but I'm going with a Frankie Howerd[1]-style 'pro-logue' (missus), just briefly. Because though you may not credit it, I **do** work these things over and I **have** re-read many times and I've found myself at a place where a wee explanation feels sensible. It's a kind of self-protection, of course, but not sure if this identifies me as either an outright coward, or one simply prone to 'critical lapses'. You'll soon be the judge of that.*

*In a sense, everything I've ever written speaks of a reckless lack of compromise so I'll be wrestling with the following until the moment of publication: the idea that the upcoming opening chapter is uncomfortably related, vibe-wise, to a 1970s toga-party. Meaning neck-deep in **cringe** and maybe worse. But though I utterly*

---

[1] Comic actor from waay back. But a presence in our childhoods. Fitted somehow, with the absurdities/grotesqueries of the period. (Note: I can *just remember* The Black and White Minstrel Show, on the telly. That's the context).

*acknowledge the possibility that apparently by-passing the (justifiable) contemporary prerequisite for political sensitivities may drive you, the reader, out the metaphorical door, I'm keeping that which lurketh below in there, as is. Not because I have anything (I hope) in common with that arsehole Laurence Fox, but because however self-incriminating it may be, it feels like there's a truth or two knocking about; in amongst the creepy fat blokes, cheap cigar-smoke and mindless prejudice. Or at least it truly reflects **something of the time**.*

(So laughably) an Artist's Statement:

I really want this book to be explainer-lite. Can't stand the idea that dots have to be joined/profundities unpicked for a readership that is thereby assumed to be brain-dead: insulting bollocks. We're off dancing with Guardiola and boozing with Clough. We've re-invented the haka and the wheel of life and sport. We're placing teddies not gifting gongs. Nothing here is a flight of fancy: not everything will be revealed.

*So chomp on this, friends: despite your concerns, I am proudly woke... because we must be, eh? It's right; it's important. If **you** either use the term 'woke' as a weapon of abuse, or fall into the assumption that political correctness is essentially wrong, you need to give your head a wobble. It's essentially **right**; it just may feel momentarily inconvenient or 'disproportionate'. Have a think. The world gets better when we are considerate: end of.*

This book, whilst wading through the baggage of a middle-aged white guy, will be anti-bigotry. Believe it or not. Its purpose is to celebrate personal and universal stuff about activity. Not sure that can be done without advocating for those damp essentials love and understanding.

But maybe that dates me, too?

PART ONE: FORMATIONS.

ONE - UNWISE TENDENCIES.

The writing? Spidery. Black felt-tip, I reckon - although it did last. Capitals.

Can't be *sure* how he got it up there, aged ten: from someone's shoulders? (How high would it have been: not the full eight bloody feet, but *six, maybe*?) Perhaps he bullied somebody - a Pinney or a Moss? Perhaps he was taller than I remember, although I think he was only the year above?

Trying *extremely hard* to be as true and fair about this as I can, people. Have a neutral view of his roots and the elusive facts of his appearance and then exit: cross my heart. Yeh, I *could* research that fade-out but just feels more honest to record the pale vacuum around how the crimson-cheeked wanker sidled into and awaaaay from our lives.

I remember his lank barnet and that nervy flick of his head to clear his right eye of fringe, but not much else; other than the general awkwardness. If I canvassed now though, the recollections of players on that there pitch, most would come back with 'odd-ball', or ver-ry similar. Some, even with the theoretically ameliorating passage into maturity, would confidently pronounce him a twat: (they have). But being aware of a particularly early crossroads looming, and feeling the need to genially disassociate from too crude a partisanship, your honourable scribe is torn between Conscious Maturity and Unmitigated Instinct. Let's just say that aged about ten or eleven, he *probably* was.[2]

Much of the rich hinterland around this has remained un-detectorised but wow; I may have pootled in the field of its implications ever since. I openly admit, to all parties, that Paul Kryscinski writing 'R WALTON IS A FAIRY' on the cross-bar of the footie pitch in our local park, *could* have been singularly instrumental in the emergence of the urgent bloke that is me. Have often dug in to the possible, multifarious *effects*, over these fifty-odd years – witness the upcoming psycho-drama – but only relatively rarely have I wondered why... and *why me?* Meaning stuff about him, essentially.

I'll come to talk about the unreliability of a) my memory and b) everything, in time, but let me re-state. This maladjusted motherfucker wrote 'R Walton is a fairy' on the cross-bar; in about 1970. Didn't see him do it but it appeared, in the park we used every day, and he was reliably identified, early-doors, as the culprit. I remember it feeling odd, rather than crushingly calamitous; noticing *but not*, or not immediately fathoming the extravagant depth of his malice.

---

[2] But weren't we all?

To be fair, I was probably nine and more intent on nutmegging Stevie Blendell – if 'nutmegging' was a thing, back then?[3] – than clearing the detritus from around some problematic, potentially Freudian own goal/psycho-archaeological arising, however magnificent or monstrous. That relative innocence may be why I am unable, exactly, to recall the precise moment the import of this landed, *if it did*.

It's feasible that though I soon knew I may have to spend the next four decades proving I wasn't gay, that strategy was simply(?) or necessarily(?) buried beneath the otherwise idyllic exigencies of life in a bustling village in North Lincolnshire. Kryscinski had nailed me to the cross(-bar), alright, but his sumptuously-targeted evil drew no immediate response. A) I've never *actually done* neurosis and b) it was barely commented-upon by my wonderfully sturdy or woefully unobservant brothers and peers. Also c) I was nowhere near sophisticated enough to go for that pretending-to-ignore-in-a-morally/intellectually-superior-kindofaway approach. D) would be the clumsy-deep anti-crescendo-thing: that I left (and everybody else left) those words up there for months, possibly years. I have no knowledge of the statement ever being wiped. And no, I don't know what that means either.

*

---

[3] Think it was – we certainly tried to knock it through our oppo's legs. Just not sure when that name ('megs/nutmegs') first came into general use. Over to you(?)

Perhaps I have to spell this out, for those of you not fortunate enough to have been brought up just outside Grimsby in the 60s/70s. It was commonly understood amongst the male population of *every age-group*, at this time, that if you were homosexual – fairy/'omo/wooftah/ponce/puff – you deserved to die a slow and painful death. A death which any and all other members of the male population would be pleased to deliver. (Ditto, probably, the overwhelming majority of female Grimbarians).

Digression – one of zillions, upcoming. I note in passing the rather fascinating association then, between *fairy*dom and what we might now call identity, or more directly, in this case, homosexuality. At the time of writing (er, lols, I mean *his*), Kryscinski, I can be quite clear, was simply calling me a puff. No thrillingly cerebral meshwork of insights or inferences; no rich or revelatory cross-overs between folk culture and orientation. It was a simple, hateful offering of homophobic abuse.

But back to The Assumptions – the 'environment' – because this extraordinary, excruciatingly poisonous, mind-bogglingly pervasive plane of enlightenment was of course largely taught to you, in school. Been described elsewhere but if you were skinny/clever/wore glasses/could or would speak French (in particular) or any other language with any degree of facility then you were certainly a puff. If you were thoughtful, considerate, or god forbid, *sensitive*, then you were definitely a puff*.

*Pedant's note (which can't wait for the bottom of the page). Puff was often spelled 'pouff', back in the day

6

but I can tell you in Grimsby we said 'puff'. Usually 'fuckin' puff', even aged nine. (Sorry mum).

In the rich generality of life we who weren't puffs didn't need to understand much about the theory or practice of *being an 'omo*. We just knew that getting through was largely about proving categorically that you weren't a *bummer* – whatever that was, really - and metaphorically or ideally literally slaughtering those who were even suspected of that depravity.

I was skinny and medium-brainy. Soon I would prove half-decent at languages. This was dangerous territory: the ether was snarling at me, from the snickets etched around Blundell Park[4] to the lissome scarps and dips of the Lincolnshire Wolds. The very landscape hissed 'don't for fuck's sakes be a puff, Rick'. Even my Dad, who all of us idolized for his manly stoicism, chipped in against.[5]

Dad was a wonderful, honest, hearty bloke who used the arguably lower-gauge term 'ponce' unthinkingly often. I have no doubt he viewed it as inoffensive, or certainly lacking the bite of the 'omo group. 'Ponce' was used 'casually' and even affectionately, almost daily: as in 'don't put that there, ya daft ponce'; or maybe 'Bruges is in *Belgium*, ya gret ponce'. Often, therefore,

---

[4] Home, of course to GTFC. (Grimsby Town Football Club. Please tell me you knew that?)

[5] I say 'even'. Perhaps it's inevitable that our immediate ether was a part of this?

to indicate error and foolishness rather than sexual proclivity.

I get that this distinction may not wash, in 2020-something and fully accept the old man was both out of line and unwise. And in a sense it gets worse: I have inherited the habit of calling out the daft and the erroneous with that word 'ponce'. I'm working on that, and very much aware that the notion that *how that word was said* to us – the relative innocence I remember and refer to – is an essential part of the whole travesty. Keith Winston Walton was a special man, known for his old-school generosity, fairness and integrity. But he got this wrong, as do I. His lack of intent and my idleness and/or 'mischievous' flirting with outrage are there to be judged.

*

Impossible to say how much or even how, specifically, I determined to become unquestionably male, but I did. The forces in play - the unconscious-yet-also-present dangers, the sense of perennial initiation-ceremony with tunnel of baying blokes - were massive, and surely formative?

Zooming out just a wee bit; not sure why my circumstances would be any more acute than most of the kids I grew up with, to be honest. Was I more vulnerable, feeble or aware than my mates? Did they feel targeted, too? To what extent? More importantly, are things a little better, now? (God I hope so, but I suspect *not much*).

Maybe there's an obvious irony in play, here: that Kryscinski's cruel, public accusation, intruding so cheaply into the crucible that was our park, *drove me* to get better at football... because that would offer some protection? I certainly became (according to Lawrie McMenemy's son) 'the best header of a football in Grimsby'. (More on this later). I also suspect I *evolved,* became funnier, or more chirpy, or more able to make The Lads laugh, or intuited that this stuff *might be good*, because this made escape into the Real (Safe) Brotherhood possible.

Who knows how conscious these things are? I may be projecting The Spurious Notions of an Occasional Guardian Reader into what happened, back then. I may be exaggerating. But I think it's likely something was telling me I *needed* to be a comedian and a sportsman, to counter-balance the ominous intellectual and physical weediness. Pretty sure that feeling did burn.

From the surreal speculation, an almost-concluding factoid: you *really couldn't* afford to be 'good', at school, if you went on to Matthew Humberstone, the relatively local state Secondary, in Cleethorpes.[6] You had to be savvier, noisier, *ruder* than that. Loved school but it was basically 1800 mixed Neanderthals. It was toughish, maddish and on the edge of anarchy but it made me and flung me together with some of the finest people on the planet.

*

---

[6] Later closed, no doubt for 'failing'.

So I am unclear on the mechanics and chronology of influences... but this is one of the great mysteries, yes? Why, how would we know that stuff? There are fabulous fluffy questions here and mutable, abstracted answers. I'm not in a dark place. I can have some fun with this, whilst gently digging. In that sense I'm privileged; just wondering a *little*, about when or how my small-potatoes fears kicked-in. (Don't *think* this is therapy-replacement: may just be noting to the universe that homophobia was the principal poison[7] in our environment, at that time. Feels important to say that).

It could be in one respect *I owe* the fella Kryscinski, for kick-starting or turbo-charging that essential drive towards Glorious, Undeniable Machismo *before I got to Secondary School*. The Polish greaseball's fingerprints may not always have been visible but his extravagantly prejudicial graffiti was most facilitating, and yesss, I thank him for that. He offered me direction. Those few words on that there cross-bar were a concise intimation of the following:

'Incriminating, homosexually-brilliant spelling, or moments of empathy or insight in English (especially), or any understanding of complexities in Maths or Science will be lethal. Urgently address, or be outed[8] as a puff, you puff'.

---

[7] Debatable, of course but the other obvious candidate in 1970-odd – racism – impinged less *at that moment*, because my/our environment was overwhelmingly white.

[8] Pretty sure nobody was 'outed' until about 30 years later, but you get my drift?

I did address this... surely? The process may be obscure, it may not be knowable how, if at all, you can become funnier or more laddish *deliberately* but the imperative towards indisputably masculine behaviours was and is clear. It took many forms, indeed it's precisely this scope, this span of influence that has resulted in this prolonged, navel-gazing tome.

Of course the major imperative was to *seem tough*, hold your own on the sports field and ideally have some success with girls: but in my later teens this absurd and often ruinous phenomenon meant I may have even ballsed-up some not insignificant exams, by coming over all tactically/recklessly bold and – yaknow – blokey. In short, Rick Walton became emphatically, convincingly, necessarily straight. Didn't we all feel that we had to? Do we now?

TWO - STARK CONTRAST ALERT.

A deep breath reminds me of my responsibilities. So, **stark contrast alert.** The unfunny truth is that there will be guys (and gals, and those who identify differently) *who topped themselves*[9] purely because of this phenomenon. People die over this. And, appallingly, homophobia remains right up there with racism as one of the great evils of our time, fifty years later. (Make that **Fifty. Years. Later.** Head-fuck emoji). Some things may have improved, but there are depressingly few signs that enough of us – and I get that this needs to be all of us - are learning, growing, evolving away from prejudice.

I understand then, if you baulk at the dangerous mischief in these early pages. It may be a provocation towards thought. Forgive me: there is irony here… and discomfort… and deliberate challenge. I am clumsy and guilty and flawed and unsure. Weirdly, for I do know that some will find me the worst kind of hypocrite, I still hope to prove to you that most of this book is about love, tolerance and the blessedness of the human

---

[9] Brutal, 'challenging' phrase. In there because it was the common parlance.

experience. From my position of weakness, I still hope to call out the Bad Stuff.

*

Despite being brought up surrounded by almost unthinkably stupendous familial love, in a kind of blissful, semi-rural environment, I'm loaded, maybe loaded-down by concerningly reactionary baggage: like most of us. (HOW DOES THAT EVEN HAPPEN?!?) The matrix is both defiled *and* heavenly? But - contraflow number eight zillion and forty-two - it's not to scramble back towards the acceptable that I tell you there are gay people I love, within and without of my family. It's because it's true.

Let's get our Adult Heads on and revisit some of this story: but you know, now, there will be lapses, steers, blind-spots and unpalatable stirs throughout. And I'm fine with that.

*

Paul Kryscinski chose me. Not, for example, one of my three brothers, either of the Whites or Webbers, or any one of the other, scrawnier lads who charged about the park those endless hours, after Stevie B's Mitre Something-or-other, size 4.

He really was a boy I hardly knew; can't even picture quite where he lived. We had very little contact. I'm guessing he saw me as some annoying little poser - I *was* half-decent, on the footie pitch - and though I remember him as the proverbial 'streak of piss' - very much like myself - it's possible my notable skinniness played-in to the direction and form of abuse.

I don't remember being at the same school as him (although Primary School is possible) and consequently find it hard to understand how he might have reacted to any offending braininess, on my part. We never argued or fought or disagreed, as far as I can recall. So those words on that bar were and are bloody mysterious.

He had that name, Kryscinski, which was strikingly exotic,[10] in the late Sixties environs of Grimbo. I don't remember any other family members; just that one Polish implant into our village, striding about with what may have felt like a faux confidence. But did I ever speak to him either after or about those words? No. I'm not raging certain about this... but no. It's a blank; strangely, perhaps? There's nothing to build theories upon, no snapshots into the Life of An Embittered Immigrant, or Journeyman Psychopath, or momentarily stupid pre-teen.

Nobody ever told me they'd heard him cursing my boyish good-looks, eyes distant, whilst stroking a conveniently allegorical courgette.[11] There is no record,

---

[10] Actually exotic is the wrong word. We didn't know what exotic was, in that place, at that time. It was beyond contemplation – beyond the knowable, even if you dreamt. Kryscinski was off-centre but within range: we knew it was Polish.

[11] Admissible factoid: there were no courgettes in Grimsby until at least 2010.

either, to my knowledge, of my father's third son indulging in any acts of same-sex provenance, other than the entirely legitimate communal post-footie-game bath-thing, for Grimsby Boys, which took place some years after the allegation, Your Honour. On the contrary, it is known that though I took *some time* to get started with girls, I did show an interest in the swan-like Julie King that could only be described as refreshingly masculine, albeit discreet to the point of shy non-disclosure. (She moved away, in fact, before the dander was convincingly or intimidatingly up).

So; whatever the motivation and whyever the laser of animus was turned upon me will likely remain unknown. Until, perhaps, the fucker finds me on the Twitters.[12]

*

Whilst writing this I've had one of those hazy recollections that are so-o untrustworthy nobody in their right mind would include them. It *may be* that he either moved away not long after his proto-Banksy moment, or was shunted off to a private school, or both.

This would imply both money and aspirations, from whatever mater and pater are in Polish, towards upward mobility. Since I am plenty cheap enough to harbour longstanding animosities towards the industry of

---

[12] Or the X-ers, or whatever that dubious clown decides to call his failing plaything.

privilege that is 'public'[13] schooling *and*, like the rest of red-blooded humanity of a certain vintage I am conversant with those ubiquitous but unedifying fears of rampant, possibly coercive homosexuality associated therein, a part of me - the Frankie Howerd part, the 'Carry On' part - wonders if he might, as it were, have been *in receipt*.

But hey. That's another wisecrack from the unwise or unworthy category. Either grown-up thinking or Proper Editing would see to that – but na, not here. Meanwhile; Kryscinski? Have no idea where he is now. Ok, I hope.

---

[13] Actually PRIVATE, of course. *Curses violently, at the cheek of that 'framing'.*

THREE - CANNONBALLS.

I may now imbue it with some weird sort of Cod Psychology – many of you will recognize this as a significant pastime of mine – but there is, or was something about heading a football. Something that's really different now.

Anybody under the age of about thirty won't know, just won't have heard how footballs were, in the 60's and before that time. Things were different. Leather footballs weighed a *fucking ton*, when they were wet. They were like brown leather cannonballs that you had to summon up the guts to head. The act was 70% masochism – plus. Plenty quite rightly dipped-out of it.

*

The mechanics of the thing were quite simple: like most sports, you needed to **time** the encounter with the ball. You might look for different kinds of contacts – bullet headers, flicks or glances, even back-headers – which you would seek to control. But you didn't just need control for tactical or strategic reasons. The difference between this facet of the game and some other ballon[14]-related frolics was that the object coming in could *bloody hurt your head*. And you knew that. And yet you still had to go and do it, deliberately and with commitment: put head to ball.

It was common knowledge that meeting the incoming planet full-on, with your forehead, was essential because top-of-the-bonce jobs were clanging, searing cranium-splitters. But *because there was a lace*[15] - an often untidy or even abrasive gathering or sealing-point for bladder and leather casing – even great technique and good contact between head and ball could not guarantee pain-free execution. You could meet the fucker beautifully and still finish up dazed and confused, or cut. That ineffable fact had to be simply excluded for you to wholly commit to the header... and therefore your team... and the game, in its multifarious, scary wonder. Meaning, absurdly or otherwise, that there really was some sacrificial essence in play, here. (Less so, now).

---

[14] Weird one. It was generally deeply unwise to communicate in language(s) other than Street Grimbarian, when we were kids. But even the dumbos knew what 'ballon' meant... and did use the word. Lads who would spend a lifetime 'hating Frogs', with significant and shameful consequences, *did say* stuff like "bollocks. Hoofed the ballon into Psycho's yard again".

[15] I do remember heading footballs on the British Legion Field, fifty yards from our home, that I should never have gone near. Too soaked; too heavy. Brown, soapy, dangerous, globular missiles. Many had scar-like and scar-inducing 'laces', for which read chunky, angular and often sharpish sinks or edges. Sometimes the internal bladder was threatening to burst out. Often you were just hoping to god you didn't connect with *that* area: it was like heading an oversized zip.

You could feel some players calculating the risk as that lump of shit-coloured annihilation zoomed towards. Speed in-bound was obviously critical, but path, with or without swerve or dip must also be acutely read to avoid either that nauseating mid-bonce pasting, or a broken nozzer. (Am pretty clear balls in 1968 dipped and probably swerved a whole lot less and less sharply than their 1978 successors but this didn't always equate to easier reading. For one thing those early bar-stewards were often out of shape – i.e. not even spherical! – so flew with occasional anarchic lurches).

In a sense you were defined by how and even if you headed. Most were take-the-punishment merchants to some degree; eyes closed, shoulders hunched, lifeblood paused in fearful expectation, pre-union. Accepting and expecting grief. Letting the ball hit. You might get away with that but you were more likely to feebly offer the opposition some advantage – 'the sly inside forward gathering to profit' – and you may get a burning glance from both the ball and your fellow centre-back. As with tackling, and as you were taught, failing to commit was fraught with danger.

Some of us did attack it, even if the bomb was incoming from a distance. Heroic madness. Steel yourself, son. Get feet planted and watch the fu-cker in. Now; stick that mid-forehead *into* it. It'll be fine. Do not bottle this. Steady. Steady. Boom.

*

Defending an aerial bombardment (and there were plenty of those, at every level of the game, in my formative years[16]) could be ver-ry 'Tom and Jerry'. [17] You young 'uns don't need to have seen the scene, common at the time, where a giant cartoon hammer is repeatedly biffing the plucky but helpless victim into an ever-flattening disc, to get the brutally comic vibe. It was oddly edgy-but-not; violent-but-not; but, presumably, insidiously conditioning. We laughed at that stuff, but also shrunk/shrank during the endless, absurd, Hanna-Barbaric[18] impacts. And we lived it, on our pitches. (Doink/doink/doink/ka-boom!)

So cruel and funny; entertainment and violence, or maybe entertainment *through* violence? Yes; probably. Masochism: cracked heads. In football – in *our* football – sometimes there *was* that cartoonlike, druggy, woozy moment; that 'skull-shattering', head-flattening contact.[19]

---

[16] 'Formative years!' What a fabulously rich phrase that remains; despite its utter cobblers-hood. Which years *aren't* formative, fer chrissakes?!?

[17] Jesus. Don't tell me you don't know? Go to google with your bottom spanked. Probably by a cartoon fly-swatter.

[18] Did I invent a smart-arse joke, here?

[19] Surreal aside – well, is for me. This has made me recall the moment on the 'Legion' where I sensed a small(?), spherical shadow approaching rapidly. We were playing footie – of course – but my youngest brother (I think?) had just clouted a golf ball, about fifty yards away. He'd never struck one further than about four feet six. This one hit me on the right temple. Shocking; medium-painful... and a lucky escape.

There were apparently cases, in the early pro' game, of players falling unconscious through nodding the ball. Maan I can identify with that. From about the age of five we were playing footie with cannonballs for endless, wonderful hours: but Jesus this meant we were heading: a *lot*. I do remember some pain – and that dysequilibrium from unwise connection.

Now there is a growing awareness of the damage that heading did. We knew nothing and there was no *unease*, or certainly not in terms of the Stan Cullis/Bob Paisley/Jeff Astle/Jackie Charlton dementia/chronic traumatic encephalopathy stories yet to develop. We knew bugger all about blood levels of proteins and damage to nerve cells. In fact we – and I mean proper grown-ups with jobs and responsibilities, as well as us wee 'ooligans – **never thought about it**. This despite knowing there might be immediate, painful consequences and despite watching the omni-present grimacing and bracing that went on, pre-every impact. Astonishing, looking back, that no meaningful concerns were acknowledged until into the 21st century.

*

Football – 'footie' to us, as kids, or possibly 'togger'[20] - became a professional sport in 1885 and the pro' league kicked-off in 1888. Somehow we Masters of the Universe and Nonchalant Golfers on the Moon

---

[20] True. If Gaz Wright or Stevie B knocked on the door, the question would probably be 'fancy a game a togger?'

contrived to delay until the 1970s the moment that leather footballs were coated with a polyurethane preparation, to prevent water-absorption. Suddenly, balls felt blissfully light. They did fly faster (surely?) and deviated more, mid-air, as though both gravity and pressure had been reduced to honour the achievement, but *the main thing was* impact was massively reduced. It was a full-on revelation but it came too late for us football-mad youngsters born in the 60s.

Hey; in Simple Times, who cares or who cared? We 'just knew' we had to head the bloody ball: even on the local park, aged nine, it was our job. If Nicky White slung in a cross aimed at brother Nige, we had to nod it 'to safety'. It came, it transpires, with a far greater risk than we suspected: I repeat, we thought about the immediate grief (possibly) but never the inevitable damage that huge repetition and/or profound impacts might deliver.

That omission of even entry-level intelligence and self-preservation feels scandalously but also revealingly *of its time*. (Not that our capacity to avert obvious mortal threats has uniformly improved, in subsequent years). It also figures, appallingly, that nobody really seemed to care or act upon the dangers, for decades. This book is not at all about the righteous process of investigation, understanding and restoration that is the football/ dementia movement. It does however roundly support those campaigning across the issues.

*

My mind seems to have a default position (or something) which continues to associate Acts of Obvious Machismo – heading (in 1968)/being unable to spell or be nice (ever) – with the construction or maintenance of indispensable bulwarks against homosexuality. I'm not sure I either dare or have the equipment to resolve this particular intersection but how about we continue meandering just a little? Perhaps on the understanding that the journey itself, even when straw-grabbingly convolute, is often enriching? Even if it remains conclusion-light.

Eyes peeled, again, friends, for the awareness/unawareness supermassive black hole interface/event horizon and the abstractedly-corresponding offence/irony bypass or *misunderstanding thereof*. If this book (and/or my life) is about anything, it may be the blind stumble towards stuff that feels honest. Sometimes that means mischief, sometimes it stimulates vexation: particularly around the limits towards which we might reasonably push.

*

It would be a stretch to argue that the Manchester Utd defence of any era were either modelling or projecting anti-gayness, with or without the warped moral fervour of the loony right, but we may contend that there is/was something essentially macho about the Act of Heading. Is that not the plinth for *A Theory?* No; you're right, but we're going there anyway.

I was a skinny wee kid but my pathetic limbs did have the knack of coordinating. Wonderfully, this did (for example) mean making and hurtling through obstacle courses in the back garden – does anybody (any child) still do that? – but mainly it meant football.

I can't tell you what made me determine to become 'good in the air' but here are some possibilities. First up, unusually, the most relevant: I did love the feeling of ball against forehead. (Passing psychoanalysts, have your field day). Secondly, I did love Joe Royle[21] and he was all about 'aerial power'. (Actually he wasn't, he was better than that, but the fella could head). Thirdly, I practiced, *a lot*, I think because (see Chapter One) it made me look tougher than I was: plus few others were much cop at it.[22] I suppose I also wanted to score goals and in those days attackers could head.

Forgive the following boast. With an endearingly modest smile, (just off-camera but yup, endearing), let me remember Lawrie McMenemy's son, Chris - nice lad, played for our school team. Chris, in his youthful generosity, failed completely to intimidate Frank the Potential Filleter from Havelock Secondary by pointing to me - by now twelve but still built like a gnat - and offering the warning that I was 'the best header of a ball in Grimsby'. I *was* still built like a gnat: but actually I could head it. That I *did*... and so intensely and often,

---

[21] Former Everton centre-forward. Or he was at the Toffees when I loved him. And, yes we did say 'love', about our footballing idols. Somehow that was allowed... and not p***y.

[22] Everything's relative. I headed a ball better than most, as a kid/ yoof/growed-up player. But plenty of the kids I grew up with could nod *better than the majority of modern professionals*: ridicu-fact.

is a story that you, sagacious reader, may be sensing
could develop; perhaps beyond these pages.

Because life is a complex rumble and because sport is
rammed, for me, with wider meanings, I may need to
finish this chapter with a wee regret. I regret that
heading may be a danger, even now, and that Top, Top
contemporary Players can't head the bloody thing. It
feels a loss that there is barely such a thing as an Honest
Centre-Forward, these days: nobody who is physical
but true and *primarily* a threat in the air. These guys
(and gals) are a dying breed but there *is* something
wonderful and thrilling about that particular kind of
bravery and big-heartedness.

FOUR – ALL ABOUT THE IMPACT.

Bullet headers[23] were and are something special, eh? They remain a fabulously keen memory; things of stunning beauty, aside of and beyond the statement-of-invincible-butchness. They felt like the absolute zenith of something. As a nipper I would be one of Royle, Labone or (at one time) 'Luggie' Riva,[24] jostling in the box, seeking out that cross to launch unstoppably into the onion bag.

I may be zooming forward further than I'd like but hands up if you remember the freakish nod that Garth Crooks almost burst the net with? (Corner. Tottenham Wolves, I think?) That pretty much defines the species. Ideally there is courage, via lorryloads of 'attack', as our lion-hearted striker[25] races, hurls, or even dives

---

[23] Realise some of you heathens may not be clear what this phrase means. A bullet header was... oh fuck it. C'mon. It was obviously a header that went like a bullet.

[24] After Luigi, the electrifying, physical Cagliari striker, who was either smashing left-footed goals, or nutting them. I had/have generous ears and yup, did raise a triumphant fist and shout "Luggie Riva" if I did the same.

[25] Usually. Could be yer momentarily hyped-up centre-back... but usually an out-and-out 'goal-getter'.

headlong at the ball. No matter, to he or she, the alarming presence of defending heads, ripe for some fearful, melon-splitting catastrophe. All fear and opposition have been factored out. Now there is extraordinary, graceful but also thunderous timing. Now there is dreamy, cinematic glory. The ball is steered, ecstatically, *irresistibly* beyond the 'keeper. And we roar...

*

Of course any time the net really billows under the impact of an Absolute Rocket, it's thrilling. But is there not something *more* if you get to hear and feel the smack of that bonce-to-ball contact? (*Thinks*: there could be a PhD in this!) If there's a crowd, is the 'OOOaaaah' not somehow different?

In the Crooks case that was a relatively modern ball – still, almost off the scale, impact-wise – and the crowd reaction was part incredulity/part shock in a way that may have been different to a thirty-yard screamer, off either foot. Ok, it could be marginal but certainly the extraordinary rarity of a header *that voluptuous* is a factor in the quality of the resultant bellowing. Perhaps the rest is legitimately unknowable and, like much in romance and sport, all the better for it? (Indulgent aside no. 28: Muggins here got a few similar headers – Crooksian, I mean - or similarly *meaty*. Just not live on the tellybox. You?)

A real, powerful nod probably *was* rich in symbolism. And when all we had was football, what could be more natural than a longing for The Nutted Wondergoal? I *know* it wasn't just me that reveled in and dreamed about smashing one in there, steering it flat and hard. Whatever; we loved our Beautiful Game. We loved it. Deep within one of its higher-tariff experiences, some of us kids found a way to burst through any angst, actively court that particular, gut-churning consequence and stick our noggins in there. If there isn't something both heroic *and* 'psychological' about all that, then I'm Derek Dougan.[26]

*

Zoom out. Consider, as you do, as a coach (and interested party). What's changed?

For one thing, it's extraordinary that so much of the sport that kids do now is coached. There's a multiplicity of options that just wasn't there, for us… but also less free hours, of free play: may not be safe; may be no park, no tree, no *access* to *den-building zones*. Mum and Dad think best join a club. Pay, probably.

Not going to get into the pro's and cons of the generational and cultural changes around 'sportiness' too heavily, for now. But there are rich, wild, compelling arguments for the decline in outdoor activity being catastrophic… and arguments for good coaching and pastoral care at clubs being a wonder of the age.

Nobody coached us much, back in the day; not until we 'played County' or Town. But the Walton/Dodsworth

---

[26] Wolves. Centre-forward. 'Tasche. Useful.

clan were stacked with players, so we picked things up. My Grandpa, also known as the Mighty Vic, had a pro' career decimated by injury in the 1930s but as a right back or centre-back the bloke knew a bit about heading. Vic played through and was then beaten by the pain but aged seventy he could still nod a ball flat and hard out of his hand. Sometimes he would hold it up like a trophy in front of his grinning, Yorkie fizzog and then nut it across the road or into our giggling faces. I remember clearly his turkey neck and that shocking, explosive thrust. Bumpff! Into his seventh, or even eighth decade, he could still really do it.

*

Time passes; it's closer now. And heading? Really not the same – like most stuff. Not better, not worse, just safer and wiser now the ball is relatively weightless. There is mitigation around the issues and there is different-level knowledge.

Probably to my shame, I'm becoming more interested in the campaign around dementia due to head impacts because a) it makes perfect sense that there are consequences to *what we did,* back then, and b) because it feels likely that because of the volume and intensity of the cannonball-nodding that I personally enjoyed, I may suffer to some degree. (Am toying with the idea of a c), d), e) here, which may infer concerns but not neurosis... without alarming my family too much. Or, this paragraph may never have existed).

FIVE - DEATH INTERVENETH.

There is darkness close at hand, is there not? Nearly all of us have experienced some form of trauma or tragedy; death of a loved one being the most obvious, most inevitable.

On the one hand I really do believe that enormous, almost unbearable loss is an essential part of life's richness – however corny that may sound – but this 'philosophical' view does not in any way cover or account for or entirely *repair* the damage or hurt we experience. Part of me, part of my family has been broken, because of two tectonic blows in a period that was manifestly formative, for us, as young people. (Later we also lost the Mighty Vic a little early, but as he drifted painlessly from us from the comfort of an armchair, his felling, though shocking, was in the manageable category. The first two were not).

The names and dates aren't going to matter to you so I'm not going all-in on the historical accuracy front. This may be an error, or it may be something about trusting flawed memory, loose and gossamer-like as it may appear, to be more honest than researched or dispassionately-recovered truth. I do hope though, to register something of the (actually ubiquitous) but seemingly epic, *cruelly-targeted hurt*, because that had consequences and seems deeply, deeply a part of a) being human and b) coming through.

My Uncle Ken was a doctor, in the Grimsby/Cleethorpes area. He was a handsome, clever, engaging man, great with all of us. His wife was the beautiful, soulful, sometimes quietish Marie, elder sister to my mum. They had four kids, as did my own parents. We were a fabulous, close mob, with children dropping wonderfully into a single happy bubble.

Christmases were dreamy and daft and ridicu-generous: games, hats, dressing-up, food. Fourteen of us at Nana and Grandpa's, across the road. Proper, if plainish nosh, with magnificent, industrial-strength northern gravy.

A classic Family Moment had Ken stripping down to his undies - white y-fronts, since you ask – and wrapping a white towel around his head, during the annual four-hour, post-binge charades-a-thon. This was a notably left-field job, done entirely to entertain us giggling littl'uns.

Ken, despite being a beautiful man, had no Body Beautiful – or that's not how I remember him. He was hairy and had a minor belly-roll or two. We loved his performance, which even then felt like some rare, if quiet foray into unlikely extroversion, though his wife Marie may have been mildly shocked. In our posh-ish front-room Ken stood up very straight, said bugger all, and expected us to get that this revelatory and racy lil' number[27] was a surrealist interpretation of 'Match of the Day' – the emphasis being very much on *looking like a match*. Allegedly.

I also remember Ken (unwisely, perhaps) but enthusiastically cheer-leading me through the end of a tray of chips I clearly didn't want. (Had probably already scoffed a lorryload). Think this was an early Pembrokeshire holiday but could be wrong; Devon or Cornwall are also live candidates. Uncle Ken offered a kind of commentary-for-laughs, where every greasy morsel was cheered down and I became the Champee-y-on Chip-Basher of the Woooorldd!! He was a special man: bright and true and loving. He was waaaay more than an uncle. Ken died at 38, from cardiac arrest.

To this day I don't know much about this event - we may have been protected from the detail. I remember being upstairs at 43 Oak Road and my dad, a burly-but-warm, 'old-school' bear of a bloke, rather creeping up. He said "I want you to be very brave" then cried as he clasped hold of me. My dad, that friendly big-arsed giant, ghosting into the room; crying and saying something mad and weird and shocking about Uncle Ken being dead. I both didn't understand *and* knew it was true, because dad was sobbing; he seemed temporarily but frighteningly broken, trying to get the words out.

I look back on this now and still feel the jarring. It was scary and sad and darkly, darkly bewildering. And the

---

[27] This would be about 1969, I reckon. It was quite un-Ken.

scale of it was weird: symphonic; mad; overwhelming. I was about thirteen. Ken and Marie's kids – 'the Ropers' – were dotted either side, age-wise. So *young*. It was unfathomable and desperate and completely devastating.

Some days afterwards I walked past one of my cousins, on Oak Road. We were going in opposite directions, on opposite sides, coincidentally both alone. I had neither the gumption nor the strength to cross over and offer any comfort. We walked on, in a silence that still haunts me. I loved Ken and I loved and still love his daughter, Rachel. But I was *un*able; lost; shredded. And I knew - I could see - Rach was buried under terrible boulders of grief. I couldn't help; I couldn't help. This is what shock does.

SIX - NOW DAD. BUT MUM BATTLES ON.

Keith Winston Walton was a biggish man, in many respects. About fifteen stone, six foot; had been an outstanding athlete, good footballer and solid rugby-player. Ver-ry working-class background – mill-workers and tough tradesmen around Macclesfield, Cheshire – and something about that classic, selfless work ethic-thing was propelling him towards a 'better life'. In his/ our case, this meant teaching (and working holidays, early-doors, in factories or wherever) to support a growing family.

Four sons. All calved (as my mate Mike the farmer would say) between 1958 and 1963. Meaning pretty remarkable stuff from both himself and my mum – particularly when you throw in the Hong Kong adventure of 1961-4.

We 'got on' through their sheer honest graft and force of personality more than by god-given, inherited[28]

---

[28] Actually I know now the wonderful resilience and honesty and quiet heartiness *were* all inherited...

or academic advantage. Dad, ultimately, became a headmaster of a Primary School in rural Lincolnshire: he bought an implausibly feeble moped for thirty quid to get himself there. There was something hilarious but also poignant and even humbling about seeing his oversize frame set off, in the bitter, bitter cold.

Mum followed Dad into a 'headship' at a couple of tough schools in the heart of Grimsby. Later still, that recognition-via-garden-party-at-Buckingham Palace thing went down, for her. (There's also a story about a particular award that 'should have happened' but for some administrative cock-up: but unconfirmed). Julie Ann Walton *really did* champion the poor and under-valued: and really did bring colour/arts/love into the lives of hundreds of deprived schoolkids. They were some couple, Julie and Keith – some *individuals*.

*

So parents, eh? I have no doubt the fact that I'm now heavily behind mad, populist BIG ENERGY and driving good humour (but absolutely not ambition, as such) is because of their irresistible model. They were remarkable; what they did, how they did it; who they carried along.

Dad's parents had both died young; not unusual, I'm guessing, in mid-20th century Macc.[29] I believe he was effectively flying solo from late teens, albeit with three older brothers knocking about. Keith met my mum at

---

[29] Macclesfield, Cheshire.

Goldsmith's College; he tall and slim and naïve; she unassuming but glamorous, sporty and sprinkled with a little of that artsy stardust. They married young, ecstatic, simple, rooted and keen - and fearless, other than for those concerns around 'how to get by'.

Plainly for them banging out a family was much more about physical love and the Way of Things than financial sense. If you were fit and innocent-but-besotted, why not? It's what you do. If, down the line, going to Hong Bloody Kong was the way to shore things up, then that's what you did.

My maths might be out (and I offer the reminder that my memory will blur) but it could be Julie Ann Walton had four sons before she was 26 – the last of them in *Hong Kong,* in *1963.* *Notes to universe*: the formerly-British, now Special Administrative Region of the People's Republic of China being a hell of a lot further away then, than it is now. Let me digress into this.

I remember very little of what folks used to call the Far East; we returned just before my fourth birthday. But the more I think about this the more outrageous it appears. When I asked my Mum, a year or two ago, why they went to Hong Kong, in 1960-odd, she said "it just kind of happened". They were fairly skint and Dad was doing extra jobs during school holidays.[30] We had lived in a flat, then a council house on the medium-notorious

---

[30] Pay was poor, in teaching. Dad *really did* get factory work or similar, during any breaks, if possible. Not remotely suggesting we were *in poverty*... but money had to be found.

Nunsthorpe Estate before a supportive headteacher found us a 'better place'.

She didn't suggest that they were a young couple high on adventure or looking to burst out and away. We just needed a little more. Dad went down to London to a jobs fayre: Mum thought he might go after a job in an army school, maybe – maybe in Germany. Dad returned and sat Mum down, quite possibly mid-nursing of the babe Richard James.

She said "What is it, is it away? Is it Germany?"

"Yes. Hang on. No - it's not Germany. It's Hong Kong".

This for me is phenomenal on about eight levels. Firstly, the generational gulf now weighing in around authority, or balance, or power in the relationship. (Gobsmacking. Am picturing eight zillion enraged feminists understandably cursing and slinging this book into the fire.[31] Get that). But second, the trust.

Fully understand that now we think – yup, me too! – that it's madness for a hubby to have the right or freedom(?!?) or whatever it is to make a decision of that magnitude *on his own*, with little or no consultation or comeback. (In truth there was *some* discussion... but this would be unthinkable now, you would hope). But chew on this. *I also know* that this was a rare love-match; one where Julie and Keith just wanted each other (and their kids) and *everything else was stuff they*

---

[31] O-kaaay. There will be four feminists reading this book. Max.

would manage, together. So; madness of a sort that transgresses our boundaries but also **understood** (then)- a simple step along the road.

The other issues were about travelling – Julie W has not been abroad at this stage - setting up a new home life and, in my Mum's case, leaving beloved parents behind. There may be a book in this alone but Mrs Walton barely acknowledges even now that it was pret-ty out-there, as an ordinary couple with no bale-out wedge or contingency plan behind them, to stick three bairns on a plane (or three planes) and commit to X years 'somewhere near China', with no real possibility of returning during that contract, to give the Mighty Vic and Nancy-Elizabeth a much-needed cuddle.

As Mum said, they "just went". OK I'm labouring but forgive me for underlining the point that this wonderful, scary gamble was only possible because of my parents' unshakably innocent love, honesty and utter commitment to each other and to us kids. They *were* ordinary, in a way. But their faith and guts and instinct and determination feel godlike to me.

*

Dad got a job at a Primary School in Sek Kong, New Territories - us Brits had a military presence and an airfield in the area, for decades. (Wikipedia is suggesting that the Peoples' Liberation Army now occupy the site, and Sek has become Shek).

I was ten months old when we arrived, with two marginally older brothers. We have stories; there were cobras beyond the garden. (We brought back a skin from one of them, and a 22-foot water snake skin, crispy and folded. Every few years, one of us would dig it out of the cupboard and beam nervously and strain for those memories).

Mr Lu, the headmaster (or deputy?), thought my Dad was some Supreme Stud-Being because he arrived with three impossibly bouncy young boys and soon had a fourth.[32] The local man kept on trying and finished up with seven daughters, or more. It was inevitably all a bit 'ex-pat', I think, but we weren't neck-deep in posh folks and privileges, though there were some of both.

I digress further but for the record our parents' closest mates were mad Scousers: 'Uncle Reg' and 'Auntie Doreen'. Lifelong friends. They were magic and their offspring remain special to us. Reg was one of the funniest men I ever met, or it seemed that way to an impressionable lad. When we all came back to Blighty, they remained an essential, if occasional part of the extended family. Reg felt close, simply or mainly because he made us laugh. We were all distraught when he succumbed to cancer cruelly young: he was one of the blokey pillars that tumbled, in that horrendous period.

---

[32] There is of course a sinister angle on this, (in China)... but Mr Lu is remembered as a lovely man, who valued his daughters... but also wanted a son!

My father (we never called him that; that would feel a bit posh) became something of a legend amongst the Gurkha lads we grew up with, in Hong Kong. He had been conscripted, himself, in the fifties and was a good fit for that honourable, maybe conservative thing that the best of the military, and certainly the Gurkhas, exude. Dad – says he, now thinking this sounds bit weird – quite liked a jovial but impeccable salute and was genuinely proud of his British Army 440 yards Championship win. Given *any opportunity*, he would quote his time – would fifty-odd seconds sound about right? – whilst sharply inhaling that post-athletic belly, and raising the hand stiffly to his temple.

It was Mr Walton who introduced footie to the school, in Sek Kong. Juth Bahadar Gurung, my earliest buddy Mahendra and most of the Sek Kong cohort loved him for that and, wonderfully, kept a watchful eye on us when tragedy struck, years later. Like many of his countrymen, Juth forged a powerful and respected career in somebody else's army - ours. As a young teen, he hero-worshipped my Dad: as a soldier, he made Major-General. We have an open invitation to Nepal, where I have no doubt the red carpet would still be rolled-out for any son of 'the man who got sport going'.

There are many rich echoes in our lives. Daudling through some family pics, recently, I found a show-stopping shot of my old man, looking fit and handsome. Hong Kong. He was in shorts and a white, sports polo, effectively in Sports Development mode, for school.

Things in my heart/head/gut went clunk. We're not that physically alike... but it *could have been me*. I welled-up, thinking (not for the first time) that the whole of my life really could be about paying homage to this great man – or to a clutch of great men. If that *is* the case, i.e. I'm wearing the badge/carrying the torch/'representing', then, to quote the fabulous Elvis Costello, "I'll wear it proudly", however 'sad', de-individualising or psychologically emasculating this may be. Keith was a mighty good 'un, as was Vic. I will always, always love and yes, unashamedly idolise them.

*

On this theme of revisiting, or homage, or fateful kaleidoscopes: Simon Nicholas Walton came into the world of colonials and cobras in May 63, before we returned to the UK a year or so later. He grew up in Grimbo, did Education at Durham and then *went back*. Lived in Honkers for thirty years, grew his own family. Oh – and became a headmaster.

*

I have described my Dad a little. Good bloke; teacher, family man; no 'side' to him. Decent lump but not, despite our childish ribbing, fat. In goodish working order into his forties; would still occasionally accept the call-up from mighty Healing RBL (seconds), if a plague hit the squad. Had a routine on a Sunday night. Would go to the local Leisure Centre in Grimsby, to play badminton with The Lads: Brian, Pete and A.N. Other. All of them past their physical peak but able to move around okay and clout a shuttle. It was social: they would have a pint afterwards, and a laugh, no doubt. It was a lovely, kinda low-visibility, lowish-intensity indulgence which we barely considered.

February, late Seventies. Because of Dad's headship (mainly, I think), we'd upgraded on the house front a year or so previously. Now at 37 Oak Road. Biggish semi: as my life's gone on it's felt more *advantaged*, as has the village itself. In cash terms, then, it was nineteen thousand pounds-worth. Crucially, to almost everything, it was within fifty yards of our precious playground, the British Legion field. Not clear who was actually 'in'... but eldest bro' was away, at uni. Dark. Probably cold. The sequence of events is again a blur.

Bit of fuss downstairs. Mum is gathering, possibly with her mum and maybe Moira, Brian's wife, from up the road, is there too: if not she is there later. Auntie Marie, likewise was around later but unclear if she's there at the outset. Abstract bustle and familiar voices. Some concern expressed about Dad. Taken to hospital. It does register but (was I denying, from the first moment?) it's low-key, this. I carry on doing nothing, upstairs and after unknowable minutes or hours one of my brothers quite gently warns me that "this might be serious". Again I neither ignore, nor outright deny but carry on, in my nothingness, my innocence.

It could have been many hours or few, before the womenfolk return. Moira is dignified, hurt, supportive. Mum is strangely composed, given what she has to say to us. Marie, her sister is at her elbow.

"Well I'm really sorry kids but I'm afraid that your father has died"… then something else. "And I want you to know that there's never been nor never will be another one like him".

Now she bursts a little, as do we.

Marie, understandably, gently contradicts: "Oh there was, Julie. There really was".

I'm not sure what happened, then. Not sure who cuddled me but somebody probably did. Not sure who fought it most bravely or cried most cruelly. Explanations and detail and chronology and visits from the vicar don't matter or register, not *really*. Perspective and even gratitude may come but right now, in this nauseating moment, we're hit with the cataclysmic truth - a truth that's somehow beyond pain and beyond belief.

It's Dad! It's us; it's *our Dad* that this has happened to. How can it be us… who've been *robbed… **again**?*

I lose hours, maybe days; maybe years. In so far as it's possible to think, I'm thinking there is no justice and no god: how can there be?!? Our Dad has *gone, too*: followed Ken. It's madness. Things are pulverisingly clear: we know things that are irrefutably true, now, about life and death and meaning. There is anger; anger that may feed into many things. He was a sporty bloke, playing sport with his mates. He was forty-four! This shouldn't happen. Why him – why us? We know it's selfish but why us?

*

Because things as we know are rich, there was some level of euphoria in the air, over the next period, as everybody who's ever been nice - or better-still, loved us – comes to shuffle-and-avoid, or hug and cry with us. Tough but almost thrillingly heartening, and essential to any kind of 're-build'. (There really was something special and lovely about the very best people all gathering to us, for us. Bless you all).

Somehow I go to school the next day, where some know, some don't. I remember telling great mate Mark Moss on the walk up to the bus. Feeling sorry for him for being unable to believe it: and the shock on *his face*. (That was A Moment, eh, pal? Tough for both of us).

Not sure how or when but we learn it *was* cardiac arrest – did I first read that on the front of the Evening Telegraph? - and we 'decide', having had a conversation with my mum (I think) that we 'really don't have to go to the funeral'. (I was so lost and unable to hear or think that I *didn't go*: probably erroneous madness but I am clear that I was, if anything, nudged towards avoiding or 'not needing to go'. Am still mildly fascinated by that).

But a kind of clarity does soon dawn, or re-dawn, that this death thing is for keeps... and our Dad really isn't coming back. However much you dream about him being sent on some *in-credibly important secret police mission*, that is so vital he has no choice but to pretend to be dead and put us all through this – despite that - the hope is gone. Once you get past the unknowing and inability to function, the hope is gone. The dream may distantly recur, for years, but that bloke, that physical lump you played rough-and-tumble with, on the carpet, with *all four lads* trying to get him to submit, by punching his bollocks or biting his forearm, is really dead, really gone. You are not alone, but the grief your family has been dumped into feels and *is* vindictive and shocking and evil. Because Ken and Reg and Keith are all dead.

*

When I think of my Dad I do think of those games of rough and tumble,[33] where either in a caravan or on our floor, he would take on the four Walton boys. Rules barely Marquis of Wotsits. We just had to hurt him, or tickle him to submission, whilst he would grapple away, giggling or grimacing or repelling the foul, underhand attacks. We were four but there was a lot of him, then. We definitely targeted his balls, for grief. Nobody, I think, was ever really hurt: it was a wonderful, literally sensational way of playing and bonding and being together. It was daft, joyful, innocent, physical: and even in this dangerous present I would say 'natural'. Even the targeting of goolies – from both sides.

I also think of the day I scored a hat-trick against his school, Caistor Primary, in a 5-2 win and when one of his lads – a friendly giant – overhauled me at the death in the 150 yards down and then up the pitched

---

[33] That's what we called it. Remember calling out for it, as wee lads....

playing-field at their place. (It was knackering – such a great race!)

There was a tight bend down at the lower end. I'd watched Helen Sitch from our school storm to the front there in the previous event and then battle back up. It seemed the only way to win. So I ran like hell and was marginally ahead as we turned. I gave it everything on the climb but the agricultural machine that was Gordon(?) Clilverd(?) outlasted me. The big fella – a Caistor Boy – was a hugely popular winner but I knew I'd done okay. And he seemed a nice lad. It was an early window into Top, Top Sport. We both loved it and we were both shattered-but-happy – the way you're supposed to be.

Dad had to give me the second prize medal, from the low, ceremonial trestle-table at the side of the track. I remember he was strangely neutral, disconnected even, but realised later that this was because he didn't want the locals to feel put out. After my hat-trick (some months before, I think) he had said something at home in the kitchen about 'my bloody son scoring three pearlers', which was a hug without, on this occasion, a hug.

Keith Winston Walton died when I was 17/18 and he was 43/44. So of course now I wish we'd had the chance to do that growed-up pint-at-a-Test-Match thing, or any of the many sporting equivalents. He was City, so my god he'd be basking in the contemporary Blue Moon domination, particularly because of the way Guardiola's lot play. (Keith had been known to write to Joe Mercer or Tony Book to urge them to hold true to the Beautiful Game. He thought football - and maybe life? - was about honesty and skill. Certainly the City of Silva and Foden personify something of the latter).

If he'd have made it through we'd *still* be going to football, as we always had, but also to rugby and cricket. We were all footie mad, as kids, being the epitome of a Proper Football Family but Dad loved his rugby union and I fell into cricket, bigtime, after my son asked me to take him to the local cricket club, 'coz some of the boys are going'. Might get a bit teary if I contemplate a visit to Glam or Trent Bridge kitted-out with my cricket-mad son, the two of us guiding the ageing-but-still-magnificent KWW to his seat. I do feel robbed of those precious opportunities: take them while you can, people.

This could be endless but my final thought is for Nancy Elizabeth Dodsworth. Mother-in-law to Keith, and therefore mother to Julie and Marie. Both Nancy's daughters lost their husbands to cardiac arrests before their blokes got to 45. It must have felt a bit like being back in the war. On the night of my father's death I remember the Mighty Vic's bruised but always dignified silence and Nana's (Nancy's) quiet retreat into shock and grief. But much of it remains a cruel blur.

SEVEN - INTERNATIONAL.

We Waltons 'discovered Wales' in about 1969. My parents, who had taken three very young boys to Hong Kong for three years, in 1961, thought little of slamming four into the back seat of KEE 418F (Ford Cortina) and spending forever on the A46 and A40. I'm guessing they hadn't googled Pembs and had no satnav. I remember through-the-night journeys, brother Jes's car-sickness and bottlenecks at St Clears. These were epic treks, then – 340-odd miles, no motorways – but snatches of sleep and games of 'I-Spy (with my little eye)' saw us through.[34]

None of us will ever forget the first time we dropped down into Newgale. Giant pebble bank; sand like you couldn't believe; spectacular and yes, *iconic*. A moment locked-in forever.

We had rented a caravan on Mrs Davies' seaside site and despite the gas lamp nearly toasting the lot of us, we fell into the arms of Wales - West Wales. That beach; those sunny, sunny *games!* Football, tennis, races; full-on Olympics, with other families, where we

---

[34] Sudden pang of nostalgia, and sadness... for the kids who now 'can only travel' wired-up top their nintendos or ipads.

marked-out sprint-tracks, or courts, or pitches in the sand. And swimming; and fishing, in the mesmerically balmy rockpools, or off the rocks at Nolton. Meeting the Tuckers and hitting shoals of mackerel. Seeing that scuba-diver get shredded on the barnacles beneath us as he stupidly tried to clamber in. Belly-boarding thirty years before it was a thing.

Even though Newgale was promptly superseded in our affections by somewhere equally perfect for beach football and tennis (but with added, bullyhead-rich[35] rockpools), that initial hit of Pembrokeshire Coast lives with us all. The annual pilgrimage goes on for my extant family: I've lived here (yes, full-time!) for forty years.

*

I left Grimsby a narrowly post-punk inadequate. Except I had maybe begun to prove myself – whatever that means – on the footie pitch.[36] I went from Duncan McKenzie play-a-like to a heads-up centre-midfielder in decent time, around the age of twenty. I wore the (metaphorical) armband for mighty Healing Royal British Legion Sunday Football Club for a year or two from about 21 and may have liked leading ever since. In all seriousness, being captain of my home village

---

[35] We called them bullyheads. Small but somehow chunky-headed fish that gorged on the limpets we dangled.

[36] There is more of this GY Local Football Stuff in my treble-fabulous book, name of The Dots Will Not Be Joined, (available at all... etc etc), as some of you may know. So going lightly on this here.

(Healing, North Lincs) and then Solva AFC in distant Pembrokeshire is all I need on the Honours Board front.

Let's scoot forward to 1983 (probably) and football in Wales. Mine.

I'm strangely (or characteristically?) woolly about the way in to Solva Athletic Football Club but remember Ray Evans, the manager, being keen to have me. There was a sort of vetting process, which was conservative in the sense that it became obvious I had to be a good honest sort, but free of any prejudice against this Incoming Englishman. (I have encountered it – it exists. Why wouldn't it? Pembrokeshire is still dominated by English money).

Ken the Chairman, John Arter and Dai the Bomb – the club stalwarts – sized me up from a discreet distance, then welcomed me in. I recall one single 'incident', in an early game, where The Bomber took me to one side, after he felt I'd left my foot in against an opponent: he was wrong, in fact, but I had no issue with him saying – and I do quote – "we don't like that sort of thing, in Solva".[37] These were great men, as was Ronnie B, who became coach during my time at the club.

Ronnie was a wiry, bespectacled workaholic. Tragedy struck him down – this will, regrettably be a theme, here – but his love of the game and dedication to developing young players was special and remarkable.

[37] Classic Dai the Bomb. Fabulous. Puritanical. Red-faced from booze and effort. Round as a bomb.

We became good mates: it was Ronnie Beynon who chose the only bloke not to have been born within about three miles of the club to be skipper of the first team and therefore Club Captain. That bloke will carry that privilege, get misty-eyed or simply boast about it, until his final toot.

But this is indulgence. What matters more is that playing *at all*, for Solva was a beery and brilliant and magical privilege: the company was great and even god-like. (Enter Nobby, rolling down his socks).

My old comrade in West Walian village football, the mighty Nobby Howells was 'famous', in that preciously local kindofaway, for his ability in the air. I reckon he was five foot eight, max, in his Puma Whatevers. Builder. Bald, effectively but a baldie of the sun-kissed or wind-burned variety, as opposed to the sallow type. Strong. Resilient. Would run for miles on the unforgiving roads every week and then take painkillers (for dodgy knees) before playing – so daft. May have been quarried, not born. Also known as Rocket (or The Rocket), he would rear back like the best of them, with his shoulder-blades fixing, before launching his bare head *at the ball*. He would steer it, densely, either back into the opposition's half, or towards goal, if he'd ventured forward from his commanding berth at centre-back. (Last eight words lifted directly from every football report in the Western Telegraph dated between 1746 and 1994).

There was no question that despite being the finest gent in the history of the Pembrokeshire League, part of the theatre around the man - witnessed by 15 bedraggled supporters, tops, most Saturdays - was the level to which Nobby's heading was both intimidatingly powerful... and endless. Not exactly aggressive but loaded with an extraordinary fearlessness and pride and commitment. And endless. He headed the ball 600 times every game, crabbing across the back line to seek it out. Then attacking it.

('Attacking the ball', for you strangely misdirected sallow baldies, is a standard concept in football at every stratum; meaning everything from 'get there first' to 'take no prisoners with your challenges'. Pep Guardiola probably includes it in his bewildering wonder-documents and training-camp Mentality Workshops: but crap coaches of crap teams have it scrawled in blood across their F.A. Handbooks. Or – lols – they do if they can write).

Nobby Howells went right past 'attacking' into a dimension somewhere between 'attracting-with-a-hypnotically-charged-fervour' and the destruction of space and time. He demanded... but good-naturedly,[38] somehow. He funneled the whole of existence (and thereby the enchanted sphere) into a field radiating out from his forehead. Sometimes nearby cattle or cars or innocently perambulating grandmothers were dragged in, caught up in its narcotic web and dispatched down the park before the ball. But always there was the ball. Hoisted, hard and magnificently – defiantly – back

---

[38] Is this even possible? Is this even a viable phrase, in 2023 and beyond? Yes and yes. Nobby was a God of Goodness.

towards yonder keeper; looping, having hopelessly succumbed to the simultaneously amiable and thunderously cataclysmic will of The Rocket.

When I matured into a decent (local-level) centre-midfielder I would pride myself on matching Nobby's cephalic artwork by calling my name loudly, leaping high and battering the ball forward. In the Pembrokeshire League the ball came down with that proverbial 'snow on it' pret-ty often, so a series of increasingly beefy headers were a competitive requirement. We - Nobby and myself, ably assisted by the likes of Grant and Shaun Young - often delivered.

The fella Howells played more than a thousand games in the Pembrokeshire League, every one with the modest heroics that underpins almost every sports team in the galaxy: but I'm still going to describe him as special.

Rocket's other forte, when not singing from some snooker table in the Swansea hinterland, was his *recall*. If I am going to fall into describing his football as 'heroic' then I might as well go the whole hog and call his knowledge of pop music as 'encyclopaedic'. The daft bugger could remember everything and everybody; chart positions and all. We had the occasional lubricated quiz precisely so that Nobby could batter allcomers: Sixties and Seventies a speciality. Hope he's as pin-sharp now.

More than anyone I have ever met, Nobby Howells epitomized values through his football. Words were superfluous: the goodness and honesty just oozed out. He was tough but *always* fair; his loyalty and commitment were exemplary and extraordinary. He could play but he might well overcome by sheer heart alone. Nobby also sits in the rare Venn Diagram that gathers in truly lush naivety alongside sporting prowess. In doing so, by putting that bald bonce of his so selflessly and so often in the line of fire, this Great Welshman fuels my suspicion that in heading, football shares something about the ennoblement of physical risk, with boxing. But is this then a trophy or a curse?

*

Language. Nobby was skipper before me. He *did* somehow seem to express his Roy-of-the-Rovers-ness *and* tactical awarenesses chiefly by blanketing the whole environment with his spirit. But o-kaay, he also said stuff: "eyes!" and "galed".

The former was a general warning to be on guard and watchful, usually posted when free-kicks or corners had to be defended. But he would just say the one word. "Eyes".[39] The latter is in the Welsh: galed meaning hard.

There tended to be only a smattering of Welsh used, around our football for Solva: mine is weak but my kids were educated through Welsh – I wanted it that way.

---

[39] Remember a game in Milford, where a surprisingly good-natured opposition centre-half asked me, mid-game, what "he was just saying eyes, for". I explained.

I'm guessing Nobby was one of about six or eight (out of thirty-odd – two teams) who might use the language fluently and naturally on the pitch or more likely in the pub, after. Solva/St Davids does have a goodish proportion of Welsh-speakers, being part of the North Pembs community, which is or was typically Proper Rural and based on agriculture and then tourism. If Meirion George was taking a corner from the left (and Nobby wanted it driven in at him) he would shout "galed!"

Our Mighty Leader's verbal minimalism figured; was inevitable and *in character*, given his magnificent, physical modelling. It's not Rocket Science; the guy didn't need to say much, he just powered-up and took control – and I don't just mean of the airspace. Howells could play.

*

We control games in different ways, eh? I had an occasionally mercurial, often lightweight period as a young 'un; a kind of twinkly-youngster-up-front phase. I was still skinny. By early twenties I could pass, go past people and head and I would get goals but it was probably only when the Great Elders of Healing Royal British Legion Sunday Football Club went out on a limb, made me skipper and slapped me in the middle of the park, that something changed.

The very wonderful Mr Cliff Winship never took me to one side and produced the rhetorical "listen son, you know you've got to win the ball for us, get on it and *boss games* as well as do The Glenda thing?"[40] He didn't need to. I understood both the challenge – to show the universe I was tough enough and good enough – and the richness of the compliment. The senior Legionnaires – builders, mechanics, office-wallahs; better players, better men – did that thing where you sit back and quietly encourage, in the hope that something comes good. Still love and respect them for that, forty years later.

It's not for me to say how well the RW Experiment went: what I will say is that these were wonderful times, times when I grew. Times when it felt good to have the backing of some fabulous, genuine men. If I have a regret, it might be that I moved on, permanently to Wales[41] after a season or two where I was beginning to prove that 'ponces' (ouch) with skill and even imagination might cut it as guys who could 'mix it', too.

But back to Nobby – and language. And *referees*.

I can't remember Nobby ever getting booked; it's likely he did. I never did… and I was a talker. Hundreds of matches, a good lump of which I was skipper, so 'in the ear of refs', but knowing when to zip it.

There's always a line. I took my captaincy role seriously and part of my personal fleshing-out was being vocal,

---

[40] Glen(nda) Hoddle. God of the Sumptuous. Enough said.

[41] Of course I have NO REGRETS ABOUT THIS but would have been lovely and rewarding to see out my footie with my home village club (too).

being a presence in those realms beyond the physical. This meant encouraging our lot, *driving* the hwyl[42] and directing the (ahem) team pattern. It also meant keeping the ref on his toes (it was always a bloke, back then), by letting him know when he'd got something right... and wrong.

You had to do this with a certain level of skill. (Bear in mind, friends, that a) the fact that this was the Pembrokeshire League, not the Champions League was both relevant and irrelevant, depending on the moment. And b) that I was (I swear) *always honest* about claims for free-kicks/throws/pens/whatever. Always. Yes I would let the ref know if he had got one badly wrong, but never in such a way that he could justifiably either use that comment against us, or book me. I swore on the pitch a bit – not loads – but never swore at the referee.

A classic Waltonian response to an absolute howler from the ref might be "*WHAT?!?* No way". Then, possibly jogging away, "he knows, boys, he knows. We'll get the next one. Next one's godda be right". Even if the ref hated you for saying that, and they sometimes did, they had to register their cock-up had been outed, and were in no real position to book the retreating player. (Again, not Rocket Science, but reasonable-enough?)

Shedloads of players, quite rightly, get booked for dissent. My eldest bro' once got booked for 'decent', because the referee couldn't spell, but hey-ho. (Fact!)

---

[42] Welsh: spirit.

You could be sarky but not offensive or personal. You could be vocal if you chose your words. However, sometimes the ref *was* mind-crushingly hopeless and the game became either momentarily or entirely a farce... or a battle.

Mercifully, I played in very few games that were truly ugly. There were times, though, when there were real twats on the opposition side and you wondered what the fuck you were doing this for. Just occasions. A bloke from one of the Milford teams once made a tackle on one of our players that we really might have prosecuted him for and another real thug from the same town broke the jaw of one of our guys. We know it happens but these incidents were sickening, nevertheless.

So there was some evil in some games, again making me wonder why the arseholes responsible were even playing, but more often than not the matches themselves were enjoyable and the banter before and after was magbloodynificent.

(In case you're wondering, I can remember just one moment when I lost my proverbial rag. There was a bad-tempered flurry or nine, in an away game, in which a particular individual was shall we say, central. The whole universe was screaming 'sort this fucker out'. As the ruckus moved towards a crescendo – miraculously, without anyone resorting to *actual violence* - the opportunity to *absolutely smash* the ball at this bloke presented itself. I absolutely smashed the ball at his head... and missed.[43] And we played on, somehow satiated).

We were in the pub or clubhouse by about 4.30pm, post every game (having kicked-off at two-thirty) and it was easy enough to slide into pret-ty complete lubrication by about six. There's maybe a(nother) dissertation about how many enjoyed the boozing more than the football, but back then - appreciate this has changed, now - the two were indivisible parts of the same, wonderful madness.

Absolutely share the wider concerns about alcohol vis-à-vis life/society/sport but one of the great, true pleasures of my life has been sharing a few beers with sportspeople, either before, after or during a match.[44]

That may be a major turn-off to those of you who either don't get sport (or alcohol) or have had bad experiences around either 'social' post-game activities or around fans. Understood, and agree that there's very little worse than the ugly, tribal violence around sport: I know, I've been there. Scary, depressing and unedifying. But I also know it's possible to be funny, convivial, generous and even thoughtful under alcohol, post-match, as opposed being a 'right pain', an arse, a loudmouth or a wife-beater. You don't *need* booze, to make your sport: and the immediate recourse to alcohol by high-profile players is maybe both unwise and unhelpful. And yet it can be – it *can be* – part of the wonder of the games.

---

[43] Feels important to stress that this arsehole deserved it – deserved something – but was upright, 'mixing it', as opposed to prone and vulnerable. I did try to knock his head off *with the ball.*

[44] Incidentally. Match. What a great word!

EIGHT - IMPOSTORS.
AND SYLLABLES.

Part of the fascination and wonder, even, of sports and the loving of sports is in the language. It can be used with a kind of ecstatic insight... or to keep people out. It can be rich and dexterous as the play itself but also thick with cliché. There can be spectacular universality (and even Universal Truths) or masturbatory dumbness. And the quietly edgy realisation that People Who Know Their Game can spot an impostor within about eight seconds can be both thrilling or threatening. (Most of us use that to weed out the frauds or home-in on Likeminded Souls, yes?) You need to talk a good game.

I feel I know football, cricket and rugby medium-well, but my knowledge and memory are drifting. This is dangerous territory for one who can't stop making 'a public contribution'. Fortunately, mostly, there's no-one listening. Am conscious though, that the slippage and the distractions into other areas of life are bound to make some unconvinced or even hostile. Even us nobodies need to be authentic, eh?

My answer to haters and doubters is typically that I'm talking about the nature or essence of games I feel able to discuss because a) I've *been there*, played or watched, and I understand, or b) (in any case) I make no claims towards journalism, or even authority. On balance I trust myself to give some meaningful sense of *that experience*.[45]

In these circumstances I reckon I can stay legit. *Enough*. I may not have 'the facts' available, and probably won't want the stats. I probably *will* be trying to capture something of the spirit/truth/poetry/humour of an occasion – as opposed to reporting back 'events' - and if that sounds feeble or pretentious, then tough. Absolutely not trying to suggest that what I do is better or more meaningful than the journo's and ver-ry conscious that most journalists/editors dislike or don't rate what I do. Fine. Different strokes.

I respect some journalists for their gritty anti-artiness and others for their brilliance and imagination. And I find myself both interested in and repelled by that whole bun-fight about legitimacy and 'authority'. Who's real, who's earned it – who's swanned in there or had the doors accommodatingly opened? Have heard top, top journo's really slagging off other prominent meeedya-peeps for their lack of knowledge or authenticity. Have felt some smugness, have experienced the stony cliques as well as some genuinely warm welcomes. People do that stuff, eh? Gather; exclude; protect; or open up.

Let's all sit back for a moment and think of the times when somebody's outed themselves as a complete

---

[45] This applies mainly, of course, to the sports writing – the 'covering' of a particular event.

(sports) fraud, within those eight seconds. Could be an acquaintance, could be a writer. Probably a 'fan' who knows feck all. Ok. Now we stick pins in; worryingly violently. Swearing.

*

Imagine you're centre-midfield. The ball is stooping towards your forehead at peregrine-like velocity and you know you need to attack it – to win it. Irrespective, for now, of the Statements you may wish to make, or the possibility of setting your striker scampering off between the dumbstruck opposition stoppers. Forget strategy and impact for a moment. Say your name is Rick: perhaps you were born Richard but only ever got called that when your Dad was significantly displeased. So, early-teenage lapses aside, everybody calls you Rick. As the ball approaches and you sort your feet, and then as you launch upwards and at it... what do you say?

You say RI-CKEEEEEE!! Or possibly add in the possessive - RICKKEEEE'SS!! It may morph into a RIC-KKAAAAYY, perhaps especially if your balance is kift.[46] Whatever, you use *two syllables*... because you have to. It transgresses something pretty profound, somehow, if you shout RICK; or DAVE; or FRANK. It can't really be done.

There's some daft magic at work here: I've never been a Ricky in my life but I walk into The Ship in Solva and

---

[46] Pembrokeshire for out of kilter or messed-up, or bent.

some bloke welcomes me with "Rickeeeee! How ya doin' boy?"

I defy you to explain this. (Actually, please do: answers on a postcard, etc, etc). There are parallels with the whole, wider Naming Thing – particularly the Nick-naming Thing – because nearly everyone ends up a Zammo, or Thommo, or Rickaaay. Some of this extends beyond sport, into the disparate worlds of camaraderie, convenience, machismo, hierarchy, sound. But next time you are called upon to power a header back to where it came from just maybe relish that moment where you (Dave), become the mighty, irresistible force that is DAAAAYYYVEEEEE!![47]

*

The 'chat' on pitches can be hilarious and inspired, but also caustic. I've no doubt there are books full of anecdotes and 'come-backs' and sledges: some of them worth looking at. But we know most of them will be as crap and exploitative as some of the after-dinner-speaking circuit undoubtedly is. Somehow on-field banter feels less brilliant and less funny than the wit of the changing-room or bar... but this could be another erroneous grab at the truth. Or maybe verbals on the park are *necessarily* and more broadly of an adversarial nature than a forage towards entertainment? Certainly, there are points to be scored.

---

[47] May need to have a conflab with rugby mates. In a crowded midfield, with the box-kick descending, do you establish authority and possession by shouting "Henners" – or "Hen?"

There can be fairness and generosity – I remember senior opposition players saying genuinely encouraging things to me, on occasion, *during games*. "Well played son, that's some pass, that". "Hey. You're doing great. Don't keep apologising if it doesn't work for ya. Keep doin' what yer doing". Grimsby Sunday League: old blokes supporting a 'young kid'. "Go ON, son. Yer magic!" Tetney six-a-sides: older blokes on the sidelines, when the tricks were working.

There can also be evil, or cynicism: to me that often felt worse for being in amateur sport. (Erm, what, exactly is to be gained, from being an absolute twat, in a *local*, *recreational* sports match? Never really got that). We've all played against the arrogant-and-actually-nasty Superstar/Big Fish with optional and often deliberately inflammatory 'swagger'/tail-fin flourish. Or maybe the former pro. Lots of chat; much of it dismally superfluous at best; the worst of it bleak, confrontational, noxious. Huge shame that the vileness we see in life is also present in games at all levels – but it is. Mercifully in my experience it is faaaaaar outweighed by heartiness and comradeship and appreciation across boundaries. But it is there.

I appreciate there are many ways to 'oppose', from the biblical turning of the cheek to cranking-up irresistible Good Energy so as to 'overcome'. Hard to avoid a kind of danger-pomp and easy to over-think this, but given that much of how we a) compete and b) respond to wankerdom in sport is deeply revealing and expressive of our selves, this territory is about as rich as it gets. How intuitively or explicitly we articulate the feeling/

understanding/need to (rise up and?) oppose may be at once an irrelevance and a wonder: somehow we *just know* we must seek to beat this crap, on the scoreboard and in human terms, by being *better*.

You don't have to be a superannuated crustie to believe (or know) that sport can be or aspire to be a 'no dickheads' zone, everywhere: from elite rugby to park football. There is or need be no conflict between seeking to win and seeking to play with generosity and style. We don't need smugness and we don't need exceptionalism. We *may need* to be careful with phrases like 'spirit of'.

NINE - OH CANADA; A CASE OF YOU.

Life doesn't feel sequential or orderly or even like all of it – all that stuff behind you – necessarily happened. It floods in and out; it courses and stops, or pauses. Memory is magical *because* of this palpitation, this flux. So I'm going back to Canada. After something of that place... and beyond.

Most of you will know that K D Lang is of that Big Country. And gay. And that she brings a hearty, soulful torchiness to her musical output. A few of you might suspect she is not your esteemed author's natural aural territory, and you would be right. But there are buts.

The bloke I went to Canada with, in 1980-odd, sent a Spotify playlist in 2023 to our Gang of Four,[48] with a Lang cover version of 'A Case of You', the Joni Mitchell song. *Ideally*, go listen: in any event, chew on this.

It's a dollop of perfection – the kind of thing you want aliens to discover when they land next August and find we've self-incinerated. Because it's *about us*.

---

[48] The lads I would carry out of the fire: three originals, unbeatables, irreplaceables; plus me.

Lang's singing is Peak Expression, of us, for us. It vouches for people. The voice is the most fluent, most sparklingly *clear* river of a vocal, meandering parallel to or sinuously dancing around the piano, ducking under willows and dashing playfully across itself. The more you listen the more you hear a very rare mix of control and luxuriant risk. It's full of blood and wine and maybe melancholy. It's a great, full human statement: I want those space-travellers to find it and nod in approval. We humans were lousy but we also did this.

*

We get off the plane, in Thunder Bay, Ontario. There 'is snow'. So much snow that we were almost diverted to Sault Saint Marie: but then word came back via Borealis Inc, or a trained fish eagle, or some other force of nature that could penetrate the massive, glacier-mint cold that no, we could drop in at the appointed strip.

On the approach we watched as the wilderness barely transformed itself; from wilderness to Possible Token Outpost under X feet of the White Stuff. It was compellingly implausible that the speck below us then in front – two buildings and a plain of ice-sheets with snow trammeled-up around the perimeters – was anything other than a magnificent, silent picture-postcard death-trap. Madness to think we might *actually land* in this. Hearing the bloke at the controls report 'six feet of snow in the environment', we fix psychotic grins and agree that we're doomed... and that 'he's 'avvin an absolute laugh'.

We thought we'd be slow-mo-sliding somewhere quietly permanent, bleached-out blue and icily dead, but we do step out from that aluminium(?) cocoon, at that weird, elevated level, in our thin, post-punk clobber and look at the feeble clock-tower/control-thing. There's a red read-out blinking at us: it says '-26'. The hostess says "take care walking across. There will be wind chill".

Wow. We're in Thunder Bay, Ontario, Canada, in January. We're 19, I think – maybe tad older. I'm wearing my Dad's sports jacket (bit Elvis Costello-style?) and black drainpipe troos. On my first inhalation – I kid you not – the wee hairs in me nozzer had frozen, *immediately – ping!* – a physical and strikingly psychological experience I will never forget. Welcome to the Proper North American Winter.

(Aside relevant to this thrilling, staggering cold: the following day we went ice-fishing, out somewhere beyond the maps. Kelly Kilgallon's car – yup, his real name - had broken down out there: it was minus forty-something as we fiddled with the accelerator cable. This is another really crazy blur but for the return journey I think Kelly was playing the throttle... from inside the car... with a bit of wire he tugged gently with one hand. Meaning the window was open. I have never smoked. I smoked, on the Trans-Canadian Highway packed hard with ice, the whole way back to Thunder Bay).

At the bus depot-sized airport we had friends waiting, or people with a family connection, one that I suppose I had cultivated (kinda quaintly, via letters), without ever really expecting to cash in so extravagantly. As we shuffled across to that shed-like, or at the very least endearingly functional 'airport lounge', laughing at the cold and the near-miss with death or diversion to Soo-San-Wotever,[49] we really did not know what to expect, in terms of who or what was awaiting us. My mate Karl, I knew, would be there. I had probably underplayed to myself and to my co-victim the fact of sisters: four sisters.

Jesus. Four beautiful sisters.

It's a long time ago, and most of us immediately went off to get drunk, so this picture is Hall of Mirrors-influenced, but the girls were and are beautiful and yes of course this was *a moment.* (A clutch of fabulous young women who then were with us, almost every time we went out, over the next three months. You bet it was a moment!) But it's not one I'm lingering upon, nor am I getting into *that kind* of personal stuff.

Does it sound like some hollow hypocrisy if I say that's not what this book is about? When plainly there be some deeeeep, emotive episodes, in here? Let that be

---

[49] Sault (pronounced by most locals as 'Su') Saint Marie sounded and sounds wonderfully evocative of yet more wilderness... and native people, actually. We never went but learned that it's a city split between Ontario and Michigan, bisected by the Saint Mary's River. The 'Su' – which I think at the time we assumed to be Sioux – did not refer to that group of what we used to call Plains Indians but inevitably, First People/Native Americans founded the original settlement: people of the Ojibwe. Then came the French. Wikipedia has just told me that the *driving distance* between Thunder Bay and S S M is 437 miles, because you have to skirt the mighty Lake Superior. So thank god we did manage to land, that wintry night.

and let the following factoids do: one, that perhaps strangely, looking back, this trip featured plenty wild frivolity and companionship but no sex. Two, that I have no doubt both of us lively limeys now feel we could have happily married one or more of these fabulous 'native' dames.

Quite rightly (and in fact with no little style) we absolutely milked the attention, as Fearless Brits, loved the blessing that was our jaw-dropping entourage and partied pretty hard. I went back to Canada some years later but this first excursion into mid-winter 'boogies', table-service bars and compulsory headgear was just spectacular. Imagine that saying 'we loved it' could be taken seriously: that's how it was/is. The places, the people, the adventures we had. Life really might have turned out ver-ry differently had not one of us got crocked, a couple of months down the line. Yes crocked. Because football. With Italians.

*

We drank. Molson's Gold and Old Vienna and other more or less ambertastic potions that were vomit-inducingly different to the proper, warm dark-brown stuff we drank at home. We hurled ourselves at anything and everything. There was one now legendary occasion when *both* English Lads were out in the snowdrifts, barfing copiously. But we *were* fearless; angry and politicised and genuinely worldly to a different level from our hosts. (Canada felt wonderful and part of the attraction was the green-ness – i.e. naivety and open-ness - of our hosts. There seemed very little cynicism, then).

The locals loved our accents – really, and yes, especially the women – and thought we were 'hard', when obviously (see chapters 1-97) we were just trying to prove ourselves.

Haven't, at this juncture, asked my companion and lifelong soul-brother for permission to name him. Maybe I don't need to. What I do need to do is say that he is the greatest bloke in the universe bar none – well, first-equal with two other Grimbarian Lads – and that it's been (and remains) one of the signature privileges of my life to know the bastard(s). This is important to the craic, here, and the love, and the adventure.

*

Within a few days we met yet more impressionable women – but behaved – and some fellas who liked or had access to soccer. Terry McSweeney was one, but critically there was an *Italian Connection*. We found out that in deepest winter there was an *indoor* football league, in Thunder Bay. We went training; five or six-a-side.

Now me and ma boy, at this time, were decent. He was stocky and tricksy, I was skinny and tricksy. That indoor thing suited us well: pass and move; skills; good control. It suited us.

We played in a fabulous, innocent daze but did soon learn that there were two Italian teams in the city, a city that like most we visited hosted proud communities of immigrants – proud to be Canadian and proud to be Italian or Finns. It still makes me smile that the football teams in Thunder Bay wore their delusions of grandeur similarly proudly, calling themselves Italia and Juventus. It's a crass simplification to say that because this was North America our footie skills were better than theirs but... we *were*, in this instance, in this place, better than they were.

Critically, and as always, in the matrix of daft or heady or even bitter tribalism there was that magical thing whereby you step on the pitch - *anywhere* - and suddenly you have mates. Boom; guys or gals who will watch your back. Guys or gals who will get you a lift, a job, a beer. Immediately, we had another group of soulbrothers. But this is where things got wonderfully bizarre, in a filmic, did-this-really-happen(?) kindofaway.

We were just mildly ecstatic at the novelty value of all this: bonus football; Canada; Italy; loads of attention. These guys were great and they wanted us to join them – like *really* wanted us to join them.

Scoot to a Sunday afternoon: and an arrangement. They're going to pick us up and show us around – the Italians. The father of our host family was just a shade put out... and maybe concerned that we might fall into bad company, not because he was a racist nutter – he was Mauritian-born – but because maybe he knew stuff.

Come the hour a bloody big motor – limo-like, not exactly fancy but BIG – pulled up outside the house. A fella, whose name I forget, but 'tasche and beer-belly; likeable, strode up to the door and knocked, heavily.

We went out and jumped in the motor. Inside was Il Presidente: (Italian scholars, would that be right?) He welcomed us and off we drove. From the first moment it felt like the driver was *Il Presidente's Man...* and that maybe he was what used to be called a 'hood'. There was banter and innuendo; we were being checked out; it was excitingly odd - edgy - but that fearlessness of yoof thing kicked-in again. Much of the following several hours felt like something out of Goodfellas.

We went to the Community Hall – the Italian one, I think, as opposed to the Juventian(?) – where we *really did* have (free) pizza and Frascati. Loads of it. To clinch the deal, Il Presidente and hood took us to a downtown strip club – the first and last time I have been to such a strange, dispiriting place – and continued the initiation. (I hasten to add, we continued to drink and gawp from a safe distance. But it was quite a night).

These guys were wildish and geezertastic in that stylish Italian way: dressed to kill; foul-mouthed; horny as hell. Whatever the craic is in Italian, they were generously if not hilariously determined to provide it. Word had gone out that pretty much whatever it took to keep us away from Juve and the other local outfits, we would get. In truth, we didn't need persuading. From forty years' distance, I may need to throw in some note about alarming levels of misogyny. But aged 19/20, and drunk, we loved these crazy fuckers.

Ultimately, we signed and were again welcomed in. I was able to tell the Man Himself that some Scottish bloke had approached me and asked me to 'come and play for a white man's team'. (Fact; direct quote). I told Il Presidente how I had smiled and told him my mother was Italian - a direct porkie but one I was happy to provide for the suddenly gob-struck Jock. The Don may even have slapped me on the back; we certainly shook on it, probably lustily, and us New Boys in Town played for Italia.

TEN - 'CULTURE',
SIX HUNDRED WOMEN
AND A KNIFE.

Thunder Bay, Ontario is a port and a grain town. Like our hometown of Grimsby, it had (and no doubt has) areas we might sling the adjective 'rough' at. But I remember both of us Northern Lads being quite struck with differences in the bar/pub culture, back in the day.

Firstly and most obviously, table-service. Nobody *at the bar*, because that's not what you do. Somebody nice and smiley comes to serve you.[50] This means the protocols around and the structure of the experience is different. You're not jostling or shuffling or barking at somebody: there's no battle to get heard. And if people are sitting there's less violence in the ether: that's BIG.

Where we came from nearly every time you went out there was some potential for 'aggro'. Yes that's largely

---

[50] And I'm not being entirely ironic, here. Our experience of being served, in North America was strikingly different to back home. Over there, mostly, you get well-looked-after and the waiters/ waitresses view themselves as professionals doing a Proper Job. Here it's very often desultory students, yes? Some can be wonderful but it's a temporary gig, under-valued by all parties.

due to the savagery that is our drinking culture *itself* and the class/socio-economic factors around that but the depressing inevitability of that drink/machismo/anti-social or violent behaviour cycle felt broken, or at least stalled, in Canadian bars. A) because they were more like cafes and b) (also *really notably*) strong young blokes who in Grimsby were likely to be *a challenge*, if stirred, tended, in our admittedly limited experience, to apologise for this or that and call the bar owner 'sir' whilst doing so. There were umpteen times when we could barely believe how respectful the Local Units were, when we suspected something might kick off.

This is a general testimonial, and therefore weak, or plainly full of holes. And if there were instances where North American Civilization felt light years ahead... well, there was also this.

You couldn't dance. Not as a bloke. Not either on your own, or with another bloke – even if any sentient being could see that your dancing with or near another guy was entirely 'innocent' of sexual import or meaning. We found this out at some cost, early doors and then used it to create trans-provincial mischief against the male population of Canada.

My mate is and was a handsome fella but we are both unfailingly, uninterestingly straight. I love to hug the pigeon-chested wanker but the rest? Na. We would both walk through proverbial fire for each other but that other stuff? Not a flicker. Now, as they say, read on.

*

A nightclub. A palpably seedy job – reminding us of home. Only a few days, I think, into our Ontarian Adventure. Us, Karl and the gals. Probably all under the influence but happy and excited. Edgier than previous outings, perhaps, but it's later, darker, noisier; it's a nightclub.

We drink and mingle a bit, meet more charming, smiley people – both/all sexes. The music, as so often, is crap. Some of the girls go off and dance; we watch. Then something remarkable and upful happens; the DJ or sound system plays a Great British Post-Punk Dance-choon. The Limeys immediately, instinctively head out. (Important insert: my memory for years told me the tune was 'Rock the Casbah' by The Clash. I'm less sure of this, now, having checked out the release date – 1982. Think we were at this earlier). Whatever, it's certainly true that we were launched onto the dancefloor by a) alcohol and b) that weird loyalty-thing as well as the love of the song. In short(ish) it could have been something else... but it was certainly a Great British Dance-choon. I was distantly conscious of one of the girls either saying "o-oh no" outright, or flagging her concern that something was being transgressed.

We had a right good dance, probably staying out beyond the glorious moment, before wafting back towards our gang. Or at least I was wafting. Whit – my partner in crime – was being leaned-into by some geezer. It didn't look good. I walked back towards, just as one of the girls, from a distance, started swearing and remonstrating with the stranger. (He was thirty-odd, bearded and relatively unimposing: looked a bit of a rocker). I heard what she said but wasn't clear about what he had. Something had gone on. There was a wee pause whilst Whit gathered his thoughts: it looked like a fracas might ensue but he gestured to me and walked me over and away.

Our exchange went something like this:

Whit: Did you see that?

Walt: Not really. Saw that old fucker 'avvin a word.

Whit: Yeh. Weird, weird geezer... did you see what he did?

Walt: No. What?

Whit: Well he came over.... And got right into me face... and asked me if I was gay, and if I was local...

Walt: You are kidding me!

Whit: No – and it gets worse, or madder. I can't fucking believe this has just happened...

Walt: What?

Whit: He asked me if I was gay – if we were gay – and I said something daft like "No, we're just 'ere on our 'olidays'... and he gets out a big fuck-off knife – did you see it? – and gets in really close and quiet and says "You and your boyfriend get out of here or I'll kill ya".

Walt: WHAT?!?

Whit: He did. I swear that's what he said.

At this point one of the girls joined us and, in a rage, kindof apologises and is half-thinking of going after this guy. We say not. We're – or Whit - is okay. No worries. Karl joins us, Whit pretty calmly recounts the incident to a mixture of anger, fear and disbelief.

It's later before the Canadians begin the explanations, or hint at them. For now Karl says something about having a baseball bat in the trunk of his car but we decide to withdraw, all of us. Back at home it doesn't take long to un-pack this. Becky says she was worried something might happen: that as soon as she saw us go out to the floor, she was expecting a reaction from somewhere – admittedly not *that reaction*.

We learn that in this apparently mostly civilized café-culture scene, where tough-guys say 'sir' and folks seem universally friendly and open, that dark homophobic shite is still stalking the ground. Worse still, these cowboys *are forty years behind*, not in front, if they are saying that blokes can't dance without a woman alongside... and they are saying that! It really was the fucking norm! That madness is so embarrassingly dumb it's worse than the Blighty Equivalent – which at least allowed blokes to dance.

This event was shocking, both because it **was** a big, fuck-off knife and on account of that culture-fail revelation. In the bars Canadian blokes had seemed markedly less inclined to aggressive posturing than our lot, but this did not, sadly, signify any sort of progressive maturity. On the contrary, wider Canuck society appeared to accept that men couldn't dance without women. Because if they did that, they were gay. And you can't be gay.

Once we'd understood the implications, we decided (and/or acted-out, often under drink) that we'd plant the flag of liberal inclusion on every dancefloor we visited, forthwith. We wound up locals all over but never took a backward step on that.

*

We went past the knife thing quickly enough – life and the social whirl was so absorbing. The weekly football was great fun and the hospitality from every direction endlessly rich. And because of the sport, we met more people. Can't remember how it happened but a month or two into our stay, we were approached about the possibility of playing for a team at a tournament in the States. They would pay all our costs. After deeply considering for eight milli-seconds, we said 'yes'.

Hands up, then if you have played for Thunder Bay Allstars. And won an MVP?[51] In Eau Claire, Wisconsin? Like I said, we were better than most of the locals.

Again this baby is a blur – again alcohol being a factor. But we were skint, game, and fearless, so we went.

---

[51] Had no idea what this was but got one: again not sure if that was for one single performance or for the tournament. Most Valuable Player.

We somehow explained it to our faultlessly generous host family, who again laughed a little nervously before wishing us well and then we met up with The Guys. Before we knew it we were trundling around Lake Superior in a minibus, with a load of old fellas we'd never met. Or maybe we'd met one or two, briefly. We travelled for hours: it was wonderful and daft and sublimely, sublimely good-natured.

If there were ten of us on the bus there were at least five different nationalities within this wonderful, mad, Canadian soccer-clan. They were fabulous; men up for the footie despite advancing years (guessing thirty-five to fifty?) and limited ability. Finns, Swedes and Italians and god-knows-what eager to get to know us and utterly easy with the idea that they *really would* have to pay for everything. They were looking forward to the craic and 'to seeing you guys play'.

I've always thought there's a film in this story, because of the loveliness of the whole shebang. Things shared; national boundaries busted for the frauds they are. Wonderful *humour*. Quiet, innocent affections blossoming. Stories within-the-story.

As we approached the US border, which I remember as a non-event, structurally but a full-on comedy-routine within the bus, about seventy-thousand quiet memos bounced around. Some to do with passports and nationality, the rest a mystery. There was a level of mischief and subterfuge but again draped in good-natured badinage. (I don't believe the fekkers were smuggling coke). We were told to keep schtumm, I think because they thought we might get delayed if the Yanks wanted to come over all officious and check us (and our passports) out.

It felt like some of our fellow travelers, most of whom spoke with comically strong accents of mixed European origin, may have also wanted to avoid too much scrutiny. I will remember to my dying day the strategically-delayed guffaw we all let out after one of our party overdid the innocence with an excessively loud "Veee are orll Canadians here!!" at the crucial moment. The Border Cop remained impassive and we went through… then laughed like we'd escaped from Colditz.

It being A Tour, half of them were at least as pumped to go on the rampage as *actually play football*. Several were closer to fifty than forty – or did they just seem that way? With games being short (again indoor and six-a-side) they only had to last a few minutes and try and get the ball to us. We did okay, in the tournament but didn't win it. Another vivid, heart-warming moment was when we engineered a goal for our Finnish superstar: the Big Fella, fifty and fifteen stone, side-footing home before wheeling away in exaggerated but delightfully ironic glory. This was Proper Sport – and Proper Glee, actually.

In the Coen Bros version, there'll be a deliriously brilliant scene where one of our lot hears from the hotel manager that 'it seems busy around town' because there are 600 WOMEN in Eau Claire, for the weekend. Cut from his face to erm, his face (and then ours) when the information is fleshed-out, amid lurid, sexualized dream-sequence with the revelation that that there's a State Bowls competition ongoing. Indoor, but *lawn-style bowls*... meaning these ladies are mostly seventy. (This didn't stop one of the Allstars bringing them into our room, late that night. 'To say hello to the young English Guys'. Bless).

Phew. Am suddenly walloped by the thought that these generous, generous men are either *really old* now, or gone. Fellas, you were spectacular.

Canada was spectacular, for everything. The thrilling scale of the wilderness; the green-ness – not environmentally, but in the psyche of the people; the generosity that fuelled, that made possible our adventure.

We were skint; it didn't matter. Terry McSweeney and a mate organized a raffle for a mythical bottle of vodka, to raise us 75 bucks. Italians and Finns and our sensational host family took care of everything else. We went to a World Cup Ski-jumping Event, at Big Thunder, where it snowed hard. The competitors had to pause and wait, or jump (from the 120 metre hill) without being able to see the landing area. (We walked up to look. Madness. The maddest thing I've seen, in sport). We went ice-fishing, and drove onto lakes. We saw the notorious timber-lorries, that are so massive they just don't even think about stopping for traffic lights. We wore long-johns, for fucks sakes, and sometimes *two pairs* of gloves... because otherwise we'd be dead, in the minus 50. It was new and wonderful. We hatched plans to stay and maybe get jobs in the grain houses.

Italia tried to keep us there: Il Presidente took us to meet the local MP-equivalent and leant on him to sort work visas so that we could stay for the outdoor season: no joy – we'd have to go home first. Then the Boy Whitley, wound up on the pitch (I think by some mouthy Scotsman) kicked out but only succeeded in knackering himself via an extravagant, ungainly airshot. Or at best, minor contact. But from that crumpled heap his ankle ballooned... and didn't look good. We had no medical insurance and feared a break. Things happened quickly: barely pausing to thank people and/or curse our luck or lay foundations for future relationships, sporting or otherwise, we came home.

Oddball factoid, number four zillion and three; we'd just sorted trials at London City, in the early days of the North American Soccer League. We'd done a little research and at that stage the standard really wasn't that high. We *were decent*; we might have stood a chance. Who knows? We coulda been those Biggish Fish, in a (comparatively) Little Pond within that vast, exhilarating Big Country. We might have hatched a wee shoal or two somewhere by the Great Lakes. Instead, for me, Great Grimsby, for daft, temporary jobs and yet more football, then Wales; Wales in my arms. For the whole of my adult life.

PART TWO: PRACTICE.

Now might be the time for a de-brief: grab your quadrant of orange, your water bottle or your hot, sweet tea. Ideally, sit cross-legged and listen up.

Before we move on, relax. Don't over-think this. Yup, suck up the influences, the adventures, the trauma, the sociological import – or otherwise – but chill out. None of us need to get too lost in chronology or detail. Hold on to that thing about machismo being so MASSIVE, so mad, so bad. Cut me some slack around the ego-centrism: this[52] seemed a way of registering a) some decent stories and b) some truths about the centrality of sport in our lives.

Also: the dots will not be joined. Use your imagination - chip in. Help me push this baby over the line. Most of us know activity, and maybe communal or team activity is one of the wonders of the universe, or can be. The rest we will persuade. Don't leak energy wondering how Part One leads to Part Two, then Part Three. It just does. Relax.

---

[52] Autobiography.

ELEVEN - 'NO PLACE FOR A SENSITIVE BOY'.

This is what they used to say about football – pro' football – but in a sense it was a general truth. That you had to be tough enough, physically and mentally, to 'cope'. That might mean being resistant to the bitter banter that was bouncing around as well as to the whacks on your ankles. Somebody was always 'shagging yer missus', or bending over in the shower, or failing to 'get stuck in': at pro' level or down with the mortals. The *team humour* and individual camaraderie was often world-beating, but this was also a hard-edged environment. And we need to note that it was, and in some places still is, risibly homophobic: nobody, even now, 'comes out'.[53]

I wrote earlier that *in my experience* homophobia was massively prevalent in everyday life and in sport. There can be no doubt that racism was (and is) similarly present; we just hope (and suspect?) that things may

---

[53] ...In the professional game. O-kaaay, not entirely accurate. But true, nevertheless!

have gotten marginally better, at least in the changing-rooms, as the decades roll past.

It's unarguably more unacceptable now to drop a racist comment than it was in 1970, but this doesn't mean that the prejudice itself has been dramatically reduced. There's just an awareness that you're more likely now, to get called-out. Clearly the Tories have been banking on (and stoking) exactly those 'generational fears' about job-stealing, benefit-hoarding immigrants and/or People of Colour through a series of increasingly depraved 'culture wars'. Braverman and 30p Lee in particular have stooped low, low, to spark division: they're keeping those filthy conversations alive.

Being white and middle-aged I could only be affected by racism on a sort of political/philosophical level: as an appalled observer. However much I might claim to be outraged by prejudice and even hurt by indirect experiences via the relatively few People of Colour I'm genuinely close to, this ain't the same as being on the receiving end. For Tory politics to be utterly reliant on brazen racism or cheap insinuations around colour must be tough to bear. It puts *me* in a vicarious rage: god knows how it makes Black Londoners feel.

*

Cricket has recently been outed, in my view rather brilliantly, by an independent (ICEC[54]) report discussing

---

[54] Independent Commission for Equity in Cricket.

access, inclusion and power, which concluded that change must happen around class, privilege and colour. This despite the implementation of various often exemplary schemes and stratagems, over many years. Moral imperatives are now in play which question and arguably make redundant that tradition for the 'spirit of cricket' - or at the very least question what that phrase really means or has meant. (For me, it simply has to go).

As I write the go-to terms of address appear to be equity, diversity and inclusion - E.D.I. I can personally vouch for the fact that a significant bundle of great work has been done in this area, by brilliant and committed people, over the long-term – and welcome more. But there are buts... and none of them are arguments against EDI strategies *per se*. They just suggest we need to do more and think more radically.

1. Racism in the wider environment may be un-conquerable – particularly whilst politics seems largely a matter of wilful and/or malicious 'othering'.
2. Privilege runs deep into the game; from the overwhelming dominance of privately-educated players to the overwhelming dominance of privately-educated People of Influence in boardrooms and committees and in the media. Related example? When pro' players stop playing, a good number walk straight into jobs at private schools... and the cycle begins again.
3. Hard-to-measure stuff: lots of well-meaning people are a block to Real Change because of their milieu,

or because they're locked into corporate goals. They never see 'alternative' experiences.

You supply 4 and 5. Or not. The point is, despite the fabulous EDI initiatives that are and will be happening, things may not change much. (But we work on).

*

I grew up through football but have worked in cricket for many years, coaching at community level and on our national 'Pathway' – which means coaching kids who may develop into good players. My concerns and philosophical bent (can we actually abolish private schools? Think they have, in Finland) in no way undermine my love for and commitment to the sport or the kids I am privileged to be working with. I am known to live off relentless enthusiasm.

And know what? Despite being nowhere near good enough (whatever that means) to work in the professional game, I'm half-decent, like thousands of other guys and gals working and/or volunteering in sport. (Most of us do both). Now why on earth would I make a shameless boast like that, in a medium-public place like this?

Because a) I've lived a life in sport and b) because I've trained, heavily, for the role(s) – including my years as a peripatetic P.E. Teacher – I consider myself a *professional coach*. These have been my **jobs**: Cricket Coach, at various levels; P.E. Teacher, Primary

Schools. I'm writing this book because this is my territory.

If I were to add something – a c) – to my Reasons To Be Decent boast, it would be this: I guess I've always been a sensitive boy. And d) this capacity for awareness and maybe empathy could be at the heart of coaching.

Now, let's get into some goodly stuff.

TWELVE - BEHAVIOURS: ALL BLACKS.

Not sure I can avoid sticking a sort of coaching philosophy-soundbite-thingamejig in somewhere, and maybe here is as good a place as any. So here goes: let it be a guide to *everything* and stick it on me grave.

READ THE HUMAN IN FRONT OF YOU

This is what good coaches do, and set out to do. Get their antennae going and listen and watch and intuit and think and respond. *Be sensitive*. It may not be a bad way of dealing with every circumstance... in life.

*

International rugby might be the best game of the bloody lot. (Having just last night watched France v South Africa, in the 2023 Rugby World Cup quarter-final, there is less doubt than there was yesterday. It was staggering, and the first half-hour *really may* have been the best chunk of team sport ever contested). Characteristically, the elite game is a ridicu-combo of selfless physical sacrifice and multi-faceted tactical awarenesses. And thrilling, dynamic movement. Plus, more often than not, a ver-ry special level of respect for opponents, even under the most extreme circumstances.

Many of us would either crumple into a heap of tears, or react with hysterical violence should George North crunch us into the middle of next week. Mostly, top top rugby players respond by getting up and doing the same to the next bloke – no issues. Premier League football 'show-ponies', we all know, would blub pitifully, bawl at the ref for sympathy and 'react' by flying horizontally, feet-first at the nearest opponent.

(We're into dangerously judgemental territory, of course, but what the hell? There are exceptions but it's a general truth that discipline in top-drawer rugby is phenomenal, given the tectonic physicality. Football? Na. Too often it's an embarrassment to those of us who have ever played the game).

*

Having lived in Wales for forty years, and had some involvement with its national sport, I am aware that more contention lies ahead, as I bundle forwards towards something that may be read as a eulogy for a particularly disputatious phenomenon: The All Blacks. And yes, I'm talking men – the women, as you no doubt know, are known as the Black Ferns.

There have been great big chunks of sporting history where it felt like the ABs were far and away the best, most dominant and, despite the inevitable envy-thing, maybe the most magnificent sporting team on the planet. They always won, and mostly they did it in style.[55] Importantly - and it's this I want to look at - they built (and made explicit) a *convincing* culture around behaviours.

They may not have been the first to do this; you may come back to me with better or finer examples. (Please do. I'm not so much suggesting a hierarchy of brilliance here, as a way in to a discussion about good ideas. The All Blacks had a few).

Firstly they tapped into what we might call – again, dangerously – the national psyche. New Zealand's *small*, with a tiddly population but the people (the players) understand/understood pride, commitment and the force that can come with unity and belief. A succession of coaches engineered *a way of being* as well as a way of playing for the All Blacks. Some of the key components of this were:

- A developmental coaching system that prioritized handling skills – 'running rugby – through (for example) years of tag activity (as opposed to 'contact'). Broadly, their pathway bred more and better ball-playing athletes than their rivals.
- Non-negotiable belief in and discipline around behaviours, at the elite level.

---

[55] Accept that it's not just in Wales that the ABs are viewed with some cynicism, in the sense that plenty of Rugby Folks will argue that they've always, shall we say, been sympathetically refereed(?) Or bent the rules.

- Empowerment of individuals and Leadership Groups.
- An understanding that *how* you represent the All Blacks is an integral and defining part of the national team's success.

One of the soundbites to emerge from this series of strategies was the NO DICKHEADS policy.

Gilbert Enoka, a former P.E. teacher, who managed, or was Leadership Manager (and also Mental Skills Coach) to the ABs during the period in which they won two World Cups, was instrumental in this. In short – no shit, Sherlock – it was all about excluding negative egotism and cultivating a kind of indestructible generosity towards the team cause. Players were expected to be good people, respectful people and to embody certain behaviours.

Interestingly – and does this figure, or am I coming over all imperialist-assumptive, here? – the role of Maori honour played no little part in this. All Blacks were expected to be mighty and modest, hearty and powered by courageous selflessness; to invest in the Higher Purpose. Maybe only a cod-anthropologist like myself would draw attention to this *and* dare to suggest that the collective buy-in to *really intelligent* 'tribal thinking' was at its revelatory core. But it was a different-level shift.

Individuals had to utterly commit to the code. They were also expected to call out the absence of these disciplines in their comrades – even in the management.

Steve Hanson, the Head Coach, was famously called-out for being late to meetings… by his players.

No dickheads: no-one bigger than the cause. Over to Enoka:

We look for early warning signs and wean the big egos out pretty quickly. Our motto is, "if you can't change the people, change the people".

But it wasn't just in terms of team mentality that the ABs streaked forward. They recognised that the aspiration towards building great teams with great people could be hollowed-out if the bulk of the players were merely magnificent robots following or epitomising the mantras. So a further, key component in the transformation towards almost unbeatable excellence was the development of *agency* – making people into leaders.

This meant coaching in new and different ways, or with a different emphasis. In accepting that players must take up ***ownership***[56] of many things, so the role of the coaches changed. In making culture so HUGE and central, so the training of mental skills – team and individual psychologies - gathered a new precedence. Players were developed and prepared to take on responsibility, to own more choices, as opposed to (or as well as) sucking up the team moves. In short, coaches instructed less whilst demanding more: 'over to you, lads. Find a way'.

---

[56] Arguably the biggest word in sport/coaching/development, over the last twenty years.

This revolution in orientation and in coaching – the shift towards player empowerment – is omnipresent, now. The England (and Wales) Cricket Board shifted their approach in a parallel direction a decade or more ago, by effectively withdrawing from the aeons of coach instruction and demonstration – old blokes with high elbows – into an altogether more player-centred approach. (Rightly, in my view. It's more generous; it's a better fit to get skills genuinely embedded in players and to offer the scope and freedom to invent). Us old blokes are now more likely to talk about Core Principles – areas of guidance or suggestion – than demand very specific types of movement.

Perhaps inevitably these ideas around culture, empowerment and leadership have become cliches that the corporate universe beyond sport has latched onto. Olympic Radiators of Carmarthen will no doubt have a culture. And Davies and Webb Wealth Management, of Rhyl, a Leadership Group. Fine. Where we have ideas we will have clones: and sometimes complete cobblers. But the All Blacks were not cobblers.

*

During the era of (Sir) Graham Henry – 2004-2011 - and then Steve Hanson – 2012-2019 – New Zealand (to use another cliché) *evolved* significantly. There were *years* when they were the best by a mile. It might be absurd to be too sure or specific about what exactly made them the best but there's not much disputing the fact that the mutable descriptor 'culture' covers most of it. A culture of invincible unity and discipline. A culture of exemplary behaviours. Non-negotiable selflessness. Belief in the project. The leadership and mental skills to execute.

The All Blacks knew, know and possibly revel in the fact that they are there to be shot down. (Is there a national sports team with a higher profile, worldwide, than them?) Between 2004 and 2019 their win ratio, over 215 games, was 86%. And New Zealand won the Rugby World Cup in 2011 and 2015.

(I've blown a fuse trying to work out a meaningful equivalent for that other rugby behemoth, the Springboks. Using Wikipedia data, I reckon that between June 2004 and November 2014 their win ratio was 64.7%. More than 20% down. The AB's figure is extraordinary, in international sport).

At least as interesting for a weirdo like me is the fact that the coach's preparation and the team culture was so strong that on many occasions neither Graham Henry nor Steve Hanson would feel the need to do the Churchillian rhetoric or the Fergusonian hairdryer thing, before games, or at half-time. Think of that. World Cup matches where not much gets said, because the work's already been done: the support staff know the players are ready, and can make the choices or changes needed. They are truly 'empowered', (so) there is trust. No team talk.

*

Imagine Pep Guardiola 'not interfering', not constantly tinkering and bawling and gesticulating, at any stage, in any fixture. Different games, of course, but there may be an argument that football is decades behind on this.

Could it be that football coaches can't let go and put a sock in it because they're too self-important? Is it a pressure thing? Is it yet another expression of machismo? Do they really not trust Saka to 'have a run at 'im' or McTominay to 'stay tight?' Has the team shape not been discussed for weeks or months, generally, and the opposition been accounted for all bloody week, in training? Why is every movement micro-managed and why does every incoming sub get a fucking tome-full of head-scrambling screen-grabs to juggle with, moments before jogging out there?

I know *it's a different sport*(!) I account for that. But all things considered, is it not a) fascinating... and b) a kind of arrogant madness?

THIRTEEN - A KIND OF PURITY: CLOUGH.

In another age – yeh, when men were men and wimmin were men – there was a bloke called Clough. He was many things. A visionary, a loudmouth, a sophisticate and (some might say) a controversialist and a drunk. Maybe even a bully; maybe, like (some might say), Alex Ferguson was? True, they shared a certain ability to command attention, to lead. And in their head-scrambling world, they had the gift of making things simple.

In one sense, too, they had both a remarkable and probably intuitive understanding of the Human Moment and could disentangle that from, or maybe weave that into high-end tactical necessity or consideration. This is why - whether you loved either of them or thought them two sides of the same belligerent boor – the two men were profoundly cute.

But Brian Clough, unlike Ferguson, was a shameless extrovert, who courted attention, not necessarily to draw flak or intrigue away from his players. Much of his life, it seemed like he was holding court; to Parkinson, Jimmy Hill, Clive Anderson, or to the universe at large. Often these monologues were entertaining and sometimes hilarious. They were almost always brimful of the kind of edge or interest that get pressure-washed away from modern #FootballLegends by the club's media gurus. Crucially, when with the audience that really mattered, his players overwhelmingly listened.

They listened because that charisma he had, that eccentric, sometimes infuriating, old-school, mad-puritanical force he had was something very special. He knew it and his players knew it. He was a genius, of sorts – a provocateur and facilitator waaay beyond the reach of your typical coach. So yeh, mostly, the players would shut the fuck up and listen.

At the moment of signing Roy Keane – Roy Keane! – the manager told the player to call him Mr Clough. When fans invaded the pitch in celebration, he cuffed them round the lugs, or worse. He shouted "O-oh you are 'opeless" at his players, in training. In arguably the most perverse decision of sporting time he joined Leeds as gaffer, after years of hating them and bitterly berating their former manager Don Revie.[57] Why? Because a) he *was* perverse and b) Clough relished his status as a Big Mouth and that constant imperative towards putting his proverbial money right there. He loved and actively sought-out that particular challenge: to 'shut folks up'.

As a player – a centre-forward at Middlesborough and Sunderland – he scored 251 goals in 274 games. (Read that again: that's an incredible scoring record).

---

[57] We ALL hated Revie and Leeds: Cloughie got this one right, too!

And does the fact Clough scored them for *those two clubs* – bitter rivals - suggest a degree of resilience likely to trip over into pig-headedness, later, when his career lurched from relatively niche brilliance into self-perpetuating monster-fame? Whatever; the man's elite-level obstinacy was certainly a factor in his drive towards success. He said he would never change his beliefs: he didn't, did he?

*

Not sure Ar Brian would have used the word culture. But he did, absolutely believe in ways of playing and being. He was openly socialist and happy to express those views, articulately, on the telly-box. Fans were told to mind their language (and stay in the bloody stands). Chairmen, reporters, anyone who dared to enter his realm, were emphatically put in their place, sometimes with a wit that was mischievously playful: sometimes, his mood was markedly darker. But mostly, his teams and his antics made us smile. He *really was* a breath of fresh air – a stunning, invigorating blast of it.

Cloughie became the People's Favourite, unquestionably, for his capacity to inspire people, not just footballers. As well as those generous views around justice for the working man he led a sort of wildly amorphous but unmistakably heartfelt, ethics-based campaign against cronies and pen-pushers and exploiters. Against *wrongness*; in football and beyond. But *how* – how exactly? – after that disastrous 40-something day tenure at Leeds, did the fella turn mid-range clubs Derby

County and then Notts Forest into Champions of Ingerland and, in the latter case, Europe? *Twice*.

Firstly, we have to acknowledge the role of Peter Taylor. Taylor was a journeyman pro' ('keeper) at Coventry, Middlesborough, Port Vale and then non—league Burton Albion, whom he came to manage. During his time Up North, he struck up a friendship with Mr Clough that developed into one of the great partnerships in football history. Clough, six years younger but ahead of the game and with a higher profile, appointed Taylor Assistant Manager alongside himself, at Hartlepools. Next came Derby, where the really special, or really conspicuous stuff started to happen.

*

There will have been understandings – cultures? – from the beginning. Clough *really was* the Boss, but with Taylor an influential and respected figure.

Taylor was particularly responsible for choosing and recruiting players: players who would *fit*. Clough knew that Taylor "was the best in football" at that. But what were they fitting – or what were they trying to build?

If the two men felt they didn't have what they needed, they went out and got it. At Derby, they transformed the squad, buying Roy MacFarland, John O'Hare, John McGovern and Alan Hinton and releasing 11 players from the club. Later they would add Dave McKay and Willie Carlin and finally Colin Todd.

Despite the aforementioned distrust and even contempt for certain kinds of authority – fakers, takers and those who cheat Ordinary People via political shenanigans or through positions of power inside or outside of football - the manager always insisted on high standards in terms of sportsmanship and respect for officials. (Remember Clough hated Leeds for their alleged cynicism and dirty play). But this aspiration towards that good guys/good players combo could be a recipe for worthy failure. Not with Clough and Taylor.

If there was a blueprint – and there was – it centred around the idea that 'players who could play' meant players who were comfortable with the ball on the deck. Even the big guys – MacFarland, McKay and O'Hare, and later Burns and Lloyd, at Forest – were composed on the ball. The management wanted character, for sure, but the 'theme' – the belief, the culture, the clincher – was about skill, composure, touch. (There's a wonderful quote from Clough, from one of his eight zillion interviews,[58] where he says that when the intensity or competition gets higher, so you *raise*, not lower, the *level of skill*).

This is still against the grain of expectation (and of practice) *when the going gets tough*. First resort might be what we used to call alehouse football, where a giant striker or belligerent centre-half gets planted up front: second resort would be 'get in their faces and STOP THEM PLAYING!' Third, maybe you break

---

[58] ...Which I've failed to find, goddammit, but I know the quote stands.

up the game with stoppages, fouls and fake injuries. Cloughie said no: NO. You play more of your football… and you do it better.

*

For Taylor and Clough, swift, passing football, played through the pitch, on the floor was both Proper Football *and* the way to win, with incidental or style-made-explicit, by expressing your superiority through those skills.

It wasn't just your stars, your attackers, your 'flair players' who had to have these attributes: the whole team did. So John McGovern's short-passing, head-up style epitomized Derby/Forest/Clough/Taylor every bit as much as the fizzing Archie Gemmill and the big-name signings of Colin Todd and Trevor Francis did. Both Derby County and Nottingham Forest won promotion from Division Two *and then* the First Division titles under Brian Clough and Peter Taylor. Forest went on to win the European Cup in those incredible, successive years of 1979-80.

Cloughie's gift (to all of us) was almost unimaginable success – think Leicester winning the Premier League – through beautiful, dynamic, rather cerebral football. He was, despite the outrages[59] and the decline into

---

[59] There were many but perhaps Clough crassly and repeatedly blaming the Liverpool fans, for Hillsborough is amongst the worst. The fella had no filter… and to be honest, simply wasn't as clever as he thought he was. Except when it came to the day-job.

booze, a purist. That he had the charisma is indisputable. He's in my book, in this section about brilliant, inspirational ideas and/or practice because he went beyond empowering players with belief – fabulous and central though that was. Brian Clough, with Peter Taylor's help, applied the rarest of instincts to their combined football knowledge and management skills. They built outstanding, outstanding teams with refreshing, clear footballing cultures.

Now we talk about sporting DNAs but we can't use the word civilized. This I understand, so don't split on me when I say that Derby and Forest were inexactly that... and that the aspiration to pass, move and express your superiority through skill lifts my feeble heart to this day. Cloughie, we miss your bluster and your banter. Mostly though, we miss your stubbornly fabulous belief that football – and arguably life, young man – should be a beautiful game.

FOURTEEN -GUARDIOLA.

Circus-master to the carousel. Inventor of more false this-and-that's than your average political advisor. God of Over-thinking and yet still purveyor of lush, dreamy, finely-tuned *performances,* from some of the best and most beautiful teams in football history. That's Guardiola.

But below, because this is personal, we're going in there via more *origins.*

All of us have ways in or tribal links to our blues, reds, or black and white stripes, yes? Think of *your* club and *your* backstories. The sentimental elastic may indeed be stretching but can we not reach faaar fro-o-m and then back towards the universal, together?

*

It's perfectly feasible that I may have gotten my purism from my Dad – and you from yours. Or not. But in any case, my father was a City Man: born Macclesfield. One family story runs that he turned down Manchester City schoolboy forms because he preferred rugby and wanted to play no. 15 for Sale RFC. He may have done, but he did weirdly-simultaneously love the fellas from Maine

Road. He would approve of the current, re-located dynasty – certainly in terms of its football. Dad played as a stout full-back or centre-back: he did skipper Macc Town, as a young man.

In smiley-cringetastic addition, my old man *really was* one of the guys that would write to Tony Book or Malcolm Allison to have words about how the team was playing. (Generally, I believe it *was* how, more than who was playing in the side). Dad's poster boy during the club's relatively isolated historic peak would have been Colin Bell, for his quietly-dashing, handsome-lad-next-doorism; his brilliant, athletic modesty. The boy could play, but you just knew he brought flowers to the mother-in-law.

Not sure Vincent Kompany did that, or David Silva, but it's possible. The boy Foden, too, and you'd think Kevin de Bruyne's a dead cert for crateloads of tulips. But maybe I'm digressing? City emerged from the shadow of Busby, Edwards, Charlton and Best then Ferguson Robson, Beckham and Ronaldo only when a certain Spanish egghead took control – and boy did he take control.

Josep Guardiola Sala. Did you know that at the end of his playing career, he played for Al-Ahli of Qatar and Dorados de Sinaloa of Mexico? And that he also played in friendly matches for Catalonia? Or that in his first senior management role (at some club called Barcelona) he won *14* trophies in his *4* years, having started with a La Liga/Copa del Rey/Champions League *treble*? All of which spells I-n-t-e-r-e-s-t-i-n-g G-e-e-z-e-r (as well as phenomenon).

Pep *is* extraordinary. For his record, for his intensity, for his sabbatical - post Barca and before Bayern. And watch the fella, pitch-side. You can hear those bloody cogs *driving*, eh?

Pep is *here*, for his brilliance, in particular the next-level sophistication around passing and movement. But he wouldn't be here if I wasn't convinced that all of his understandings and his practice are not just built upon theoretical/strategic wizardry... but upon skills. He gets the most skillful players. Players – like Stones – who have more touch, time and awareness than their competitors – than centre-halves are supposed to have.[60]

Guardiola both hoovers up and *develops* footballers who can 'step in' because they have the ball under their will. He's *in the business* of celebrating and vindicating skills: making the world better through the non-forces of touch and control.

*

There are negatives in play. Significantly so. The money behind City and the regime(s) behind that money are in the Obscenely Beyond the Pale[61] department. I have no issue with anyone who cannot abide Manchester City (or Newcastle, etc, etc) for their direct links to whatever

---

[60] John Stones is nominally a centre-back – or was. But the lad can cruise in midfield. Has the necessary touch.

[61] Wow. Speaking as someone who used chestnut pale fencing a thousand times in my many years in landscaping work, it's kinda lovely to check on the derivation of that phrase...

foulness offends them the most. Make the arguments. I accept we need to register an asterisk against all of the City/Pep positives and note the near-certain abuses against Financial Fair Play that the club's lawyers are repeatedly kicking out into the conveniently distant future.

Football admin's reputation for clunky incompetence and/or outright corruption may be further despoiling itself. Only we're not seeing it, because of the strategic delays being forced by City's army of lawyers. There is no justice; us fans don't expect any. The theoretical enormity of the things at stake – points deductions? Stripping titles? – weigh heavily against the exorcise of that which is right, fair and explicit under the laws. The Lawyers for the Blue Moon will distract and delay so long that any crimes will feel historical to the point of irrelevance. Thus City (and the rest) are or will be Protected Species.

*

But back to those positives – of which there are many. Guardiola shifted things, made it possible for David Silva to twinkle in a Premier League that was (his kind of) twinkle-resistant for so long, previously. How? By threading those silken skills right through his team; by making them better than everyone else. By *out-playing* the other fekkers.

Silva D became the most beautiful and most influential player in the league because Guardiola's carousel was so fabulous and smart and swift and skillful that even teams packed with attritional donkeys couldn't stifle or out-muscle them. They were so good that your Burnleys or Evertons almost never got close. Nobody, really, could 'get in amongst' City. You can't attack a ball that's just been slid past you, into that space, that Mahrez just invented. And now look: fucking De Bruyne!

It may be that Pep's wizardry has certain commonalities with Clough's. But the Derby and Forest man's visceral personal charisma burned more fiercely and was more cardinal to the project. (Guardiola is no full-on geek but it might be fair to say that his principal drivers spring forth from irresistible, indeed captivating tactical revelations. His players love him for his mind... and because they have to).

Clough, famously, laid out a towel in the dressing room and placed a ball on it. Like some mesmeric Druid symbol. During matches, his team talk might consist of little more than:

"See that? The ball. That's what **we** play with. Go out and get it, gentlemen".

Because of the work done over the previous weeks and months, and because of the blend of brilliance and guts in Clough's teams, this was enough. The near-wild gaffer's genius was to establish an extraordinary belief and empowerment in the players. In a way, it was simple. Guardiola is different – the times are different.

*

Some argue that there may no longer be such a thing as a *formation*, in modern footie. Things are just too fluid. Others point us back to alleged similarities between what City are doing/have done and the 1920-30s Gooners.

It may not be accurate to ascribe the introduction of the WM system to Herbert Chapman, at Arsenal, but it's widely accepted that it was **boss**, during that period. Fascinatingly, the two-letter-five-man structure may have directly inspired Guardiola – or certainly the option for 3-2-2-3 can be drawn from there.

(OK. Anorak on, briefly. Picture the M as defenders, the W as attackers. Each point being a player. Don't get too bogged down in the names, they have always changed. Lower points of the M could be left back, centre-back, right back. Apexes left and right half. The two lower points of the W could be inside left and right, with the three-pronged attack being left wing, centre-forward, right wing).

Importantly, there are a) three defenders and b) four players playing central, between the penalty boxes. This is very Guardiola; particularly the notion of a *controlling box* in midfield. Naturally, our Catalan friend has jazzed this up – and then some. For one thing, back in the day, these roles were relatively fixed; they really were *positions*. Now it's not just Pep whose head is fizzing with rotations and options-into-space.

Chapman and his rivals had been spurred towards their revolution by a change in the offside law. When he died (in post) in 1934, the strangely unsung George Allinson continued Arsenal's dominance into a rather Pep-like dynasty. There's a fabulous thesis awaiting somebody on the subject of whether these Arsenal and City phenomena are the only eras so-o dependent upon *tactical sparkle*. (I'm thinking Liverpool and United were more about congenital, hard-driven energy but this could be total cobblers).

Whatever. How wonderful that we might even consider, even in the abstract, that a 100 year-old formation *may be* being used as a springboard towards tactical advantage now? In the case of City, *we have seen* the three (relatively) central defenders with two false fullbacks. We have seen Stones (for one) 'stepping in' and Gundogan or one of the Silvas sniffing out the half-spaces further forward. Overloads are the modern manifestation of that historical aspiration for 'spare men'. Everybody looks to that. But essential to the Guardiola schtick is the fluidity, the variation, the multiplicity of ways his teams can hurt you.

The 3-2-2-3 can be 4-2-3-1 or there may even be no out-and-out striker. Or the false full-backs may be more like wing-backs. Increasingly, with the game being utterly in thrall to the idea that you must draw your opposition in, before exposing space behind, 'keepers may be the central point in the theoretical M (or alternative defensive system), effectively making them 'outfield players'. It may look reckless and scare the life out of supporters but goalies and deep defenders cultivate – i.e. practice – the offering of angles and the necessary comfort in possession for endless hours, in order to **'play through the press'**. Even international class defenders could not contemplate doing anything this dangerous – this reliant upon ball-skills – until about five years ago. Now it's *de rigeur*.

This is Pep's territory, his obsession. The unpicking of the opposition by engineering space and threading passes in to players timing their runs. (There are interviews where Guardiola effuses about precisely this and signals how instrumental this is to the City Way. Gundogan, unsurprisingly, often figures as an example of Peak Pep, in these illuminations[62]).

Better pitches, better athletes and a baseline increase in tactical awareness amongst players that Clough, never mind Chapman could barely imagine have all contributed to this era of Pep, Klopp, Tüchel and Arteta. Guys who share the frenzy. Their fanaticism for tactical supremacy is a) sometimes plain unattractive and b) may even feel as important as taking the three points, Brian. All four can be arseholes on the touchline – and no, the 'pressure' is no excuse for that – but they have entertained us with some of the greatest club football the world has ever seen. It's a marginal call but for me Guardiola edges it, aesthetically.

*

---

[62] Inevitably, time and players move on. *This week*, Guardiola's circus-master was Bernardo Silva, as they slaughtered MU at Old Trafford.

To unzip Chelsea, Arsenal or Milan, the City staff – we have to accept this is a group effort, yes? – get into barely comprehensible ridicu-detail. Indeed they do this every week. Stats; video; 'game-prep'. I like to think that whilst they do, of course, account for the opposition's strengths and weaknesses they spend longer honing their own, mercurial merry-go-round. Rehearsing and refining their moves; improving their barely-improvable skills. Hard to know but please god let their brilliance be at least *marginally* more about joyful, instinctive artistry than passages learned by rote. (We know it must be both).

There is the suggestion that Guardiola's incredible attention to potential tactical advantages spills over into indulgence. (Why wouldn't it? If winning has become so easy, why wouldn't the maestro seek additional ways to gratify his urges?) This we can both understand and call out for its madness, should it cost a Champions League title or two.

Guardiola is guilty of that; disappearing so far up his own bottie (in the search for greatness *and* satisfaction?) that his team lost MASSIVE GAMES that a Typical City Performance would have surely won. But no; Josep wanted the world to see another undeniable masterstroke… and fell upon that sword. His manoeuvres can be everything: this *has* been a weakness.

*

We often resort to game-of-chess imagery, when contemplating elite football: this makes sense, yes, when thinking of Manchester City and their gorgeous but densely strategic patterns? Whether we've heard about or felt Grealish's shock, having been catapulted into the Pepzone, there to discover an unthinkably higher level of tactical awareness and responsibility, or not, we fans smell the intensity and the culture-of-rehearsal, of 'moves'. Grealish can play, but the word is he was *seriously challenged* by the expectations around learning and/or effecting killer moves, post that transfer from Villa.

Which brings us to another edge. Guardiola is ruthlessly crystalline about squad competition. No buts: if you don't perform there will be somebody there to rob your place. Somehow I quite like the brutal clashing of that fascistic clarity against the sophistication elsewhere. ('No place for a sensitive boy', anybody?)

City's success may be predicated on the manager's cerebral/tactical qualities but their resources *have* made luxurious depth possible. This means players absolutely on their mettle... but it also means disappointments. The gaffer publicly and actively encourages grown-up acceptance of the Battle for Places, but how this goes down with a squad full of genuine superstars is hard to gauge.

The management of Big Name Players may not have changed much, despite our concerns that egos have exponentially expanded. How many though, are likely to find a biggish dollop of humility, and thereby buy in to the huge demands on their professional attention? How many sulk and disappear? It feels like most either knuckle down or silently capitulate: they know that they only stay in this team – Manchester City, the best club side in the world over the last several years – by doing the job. This does mean *learning:* listening to Pep.

Guardiola's critics, or those who would re-calibrate his achievements, will and do suggest that he has only been so extraordinarily dominant because of the financial resources made available to him by giant clubs like Bayern, Barcelona and now City. They are all, or were all swimming in money.

Klopp, they argue, pound for pound, is as good, or better, given the zillions less spent at Liverpool. Decent point, but Pep would also make a Sunday League team better, with his intelligence and drive and understanding of shape and space.[63] However the *nature* of his teams – that beautiful carousel, that bewildering dynamism – is only possible with superb raw materials. He does draw in the best players - of course he bloody does!

As a human, you suspect Guardiola may be more approachable than say Clough or Ferguson on matters of selection or strategy but the imagined absence of bawled rebuttals or fearsome hairdryers doesn't necessarily mean relationships are easier. I'm guessing that prima donnas do get short shrift, or just don't feel they can argue with Guardiola's judgement, on account

---

[63] Klopp would, too, yes? In fact there is a sense in which Klopp's more immediate cordiality and propensity to man-hug may equip him better for the mortal realm. We'll probably never know.

of his irrefutably gobsmacking record. Discipline rarely seems to be a problem, under Pep.

*

A brief return into coach/management theory. Because yaknow, *sport development*.

It appears, from the relentless signaling and coaching from the sidelines, that Guardiola (and the rest) either cannot still their nervous energy, or that they feel they have to continuously instruct players on apparently critical readjustments. Again I wonder aloud whether this is necessary: should they not, instead, be preparing their players better and more fully towards owning match-situations, 'live', themselves?

Therefore... questions:

- Is this more about the manager's nervous energy than any need to instruct?
- Is it 84% macho posturing?
- Is it a kind of inertia – it's always been done, so...?
- Does it *help*, this mania, this 'urgency?' Does it *grow leaders*?
- How does it fit with the universal (coaching) shift towards player empowerment and player development?
- Does it help – will it make your team more likely to win – if you fill a substitute's head with 43 Things to Think About eight seconds before he/she runs on? (Didn't you work on this stuff before? Don't you trust him/her?)

• HOW NECESSARY IS ALL THIS bawling and pointing and 'direction?' In a team full of elite professional athletes who've been working all week/ all their sentient lives, on this football-thing?

Perhaps this is unrealistic; or perhaps I slander or underestimate the great football coaches of the current day, who virtually all do 'chip in' more or less manically from the touchlines.

But yaknow. Wouldn't mind hearing the view of Graham Henry.

*

And finally.

It would be a travesty to suggest that WM is once again the go-to strategy for leading club and international sides *but* the (3-2-2-3 /4-2- 'you other lot rotate!') featuring a midfield *controlling box* element of four central players – 2 essentially defensive, 2 box-to-box - feels quite Pep. Plainly his teams are not only more liberated, more sophisticated than those pioneering tacticians, they are ahead of the current pack. Witness the innovations, the 'false' components, whether they be at full-back or further up the park. Modern extrapolations in response to improved conditions and awareness.

Guardiola's teams caress and nurture the ball and slide into space: they surpass physicality. They appear around you. Intrinsic to them is the expression of a kind of grace. I wholly approve of this part of the project - the supremacy of skills. Seeing Man City play and succeed *as they do* is like some (admittedly rather isolated) vindication of human evolution. Respect.

FIFTEEN - (Don't mention the) BAZBALL.

Who knew that one of The Great Stimuli could be that cerebrotastic dichotomy between super-sophisticated generosity – results don't matter, entertainment does - and my specialist subject, dumb machismo? Who knew it could be so gloriously and inkily imprinted into the national consciousness by two blokes born in New Zealand, now blazing a comet-like trail for Ingerland (and Wales) *Cricket?!?*

Answer? EVERYBODY KNOWS. Coz Stokes and McCullum. And **Bazball.**

The lads from Christchurch and Dunedin respectively dun gud, have they not? (As well as *doing good?*) In fact their goodness has been central to the gudness. That is, their capacity to blast us into the arms of the clickbait generation *has been predicated*, arguably, on generosity. The era of Tik-Tok and the gif, which has deeply informed and even re-calibrated the game, **fits** with their irresistible urgency. Or vice-versa. But to the glitzy cynicism of the world of 'socials', This England has added a little wonder.

There's been a boom in both excitement and liberation. Test Cricket, potentially the crustiest, most regally exclusive enclave – and therefore viewed as excitement and liberation-lite by many - became cool. Ho-ly shit and *shock-horror face*, even Australians have confessed that England have been stirringly good to watch, and that some of the Stokes-McCullum cultural-environment-stuff has been truly excellent.[64]

*

Given that this book may yet prove to be about how life and activity can be twin streams, dancing and co-mingling, perhaps it might be wise to dabble briefly with some potentially relevant family &/or background stuff on our dashing, transforming heroes?

Stokes has Māori heritage on his mother's side, and bares a tattoo in recognition. He qualifies for England and Wales having lived in Cockermouth, in the North, from the age of twelve. Wikipedia reckons he left Cockermouth School – state, not private – with a single GCSE, in P.E. But aged fifteen he was already looking a serious candidate for professional sport, being part of the Cockermouth CC side that won the local Premier Cricket League. He signed for Durham. Ben has brothers, and his parents opted to return to live in New Zealand in 2013.

Father Ged Stokes had been appointed Head Coach of Workington Town rugby league club, in 2003. It may

---

[64] But there are buts? Mine – not those teeth-gritting Aussies. More on this later.

not be unreasonable, therefore to project the following, into the family situation:

- That sparkling river of sporting confidence.
- Discussion of skills/tactics/coaching.
- (Maybe) some understanding of *what it takes* – in terms of technique(s), commitment, honour and toughness?

Revealingly, perhaps, the only information readily available about Deborah Stokes[65] – Ben's mother – relates to the Māori connection and the court case against the Sun, which published a hugely distressing story on its front page, in September 2019. Later that appalling rag paid substantial damages and conceded the story should not have been published.

Ben Stokes's personal life has been pored over elsewhere. He's had some scrapes. I wonder how many of us who may have had concerns about him have been rather surprised to find him speak with such intelligence and even erudition about everything from cricket to mental health? He seems a top-notch fella.

His career in cricket sends yer average statty into a masturbatory frenzy. It's heroic and sensational and yes, legendary. I'm just gonna drop in some boring factoids.

---

[65] Dig deepish and you will find that she 'was a renowned cricketer in New Zealand'.

- April 2022, he succeeded Joe Roooot as England Test skipper, under the new coach Bazza.
- May 2022, making a rare appearance for Durham, he struck five consecutive sixes against Worcestershire, before missing out on a share of the iconic record by miscuing the last ball for four.
- In Feb 2023 he set the record for number of sixes struck in a Test career, beating one B B McCullum's tally of 107.
- England: the man wins games – series, trophies – on his own.
- There is something godlike about him: he even looks a bit like a bearded god. With tattoos.
- Brendon Barrie, like Benjamin Andrew, *has something*. Like his skipper, he's an extraordinary record-breaker and those records tend to have been about explosivity – the most or quickest, etc, etc. As a player he was a brilliant, often alarmingly pro-active high order bat who captained his country then swung that willow around the universe as one of the earliest globe-trotting, franchise-hopping gladiators/mercenaries/#legends. (Delete according to prejudices/tribal loyalties/closeness with the Righteous History of the Game).

Almost everybody loved McCullum for his fearlessness, but it may be fair to say that his later career polarized opinion, or ushered in some of the debate about mercenaries/franchises/'circuses'. McCullum played for the following, as well as Otago, Canterbury and New Zealand: (with apologies to our friends at Wikipedia).

2006	Glamorgan
• 2008–2010 • 2012–2013	Kolkata Knight Riders
2008/09	New South Wales
2010	Sussex
2011	Kochi Tuskers Kerala
2011/12–2018/19	Brisbane Heat
2014–2015	Chennai Super Kings
2015	Warwickshire
2016–2017	Gujarat Lions
2016–2017	Middlesex
2016–2018	Trinbago Knight Riders
2017–2018	Lahore Qalandars
2017	Rangpur Riders
2018	Royal Challengers Bangalore
2018	Kandahar Knights

Somehow, it was Rob Key, the former England player and respected, affable pundit, who ushered in the new era. Stokes and McCullum may have been mates of his as much as candidates – the latter had no experience of coaching at Test level. In a way all three fell into a vacuum ripe for change and innovation. The 'selection process' for the various roles may have been three parts golf, two parts 'beers'. A year later nobody cared.

Barely credibly, Stokes and McCullum brought talking a good game to a whole new level… and then delivered. They *actually did say* publicly that entertaining people was more important than results. (In. Test. Cricket). They *actually did seem to believe* that

Zak Crawley *should* go after the bowling from the first delivery. (He did, with mixed fortunes, but the rate at which England scored runs bolted unthinkably). They kept on winning - *in Tests* - whilst slashing and carving the ball relentlessly around the park.

It was undeniable in theory and in practice: a historic shift. Test Cricket had been changed and possibly saved. Bazza and Stokesy are *here* because their re-invigoration of long-form cricket was and is empirically and philosophically fabulous. The level or quality of horny machismo involved may be irrelevant, given the sheer pleasure England delivered: but we need to look at it – and some of the issues that remain, for cricket.

*

There is a clear danger of underestimating Stokes and McCullum, who are both engaging and deeply thoughtful men, because of the fug of laddishness that they operate in or through. But despite the banter, beers, squad six-hitting contests[66] and the driven, possibly flawed or over-simplified method, these guys have nailed something refreshing and genuinely resonant. Some will judge that this places them beyond criticism.

They probably recognize that the man-hug heavy, positivity-loaded team humour *could* breed so much machismo that poor decisions are made in the name of freedom. (Some would argue that this was inevitable... and that it's happened). They probably understand that

---

[66] Famously won by the coach...

although we all reach for positivity and for the free expression of skills, there have to be limits – or at least 'smart cricket' has to intrude, given the moment.

Or maybe not? Maybe they do think it really is as simple as practicing processes and then letting go of all the things that mitigate against belief in the positive? Letting go of match strategy, or state of play, or time, and just releasing an endless flow of alacrity. Maybe there's not just a kind of power in that but a kind of grace? This England won games and lost games but their gun-sticking was relentlessly convincing and ver-ry successful. The batting was and remains gobsmacking, statistically – the rate of scoring being double the traditional rate of a decade ago.[67] Maybe we should just stand the fuck up and applaud them to the boundary?

It is and it isn't that simple. The following may all be true:

- Since Brendon Barrie McCullum and Benjamin Andrew Stokes took over the realms[68] at England, the world of Test Cricket got better.
- And the world of sport.
- And the world.
- Their leadership, being about positivity and belief and trust, sets a kind of exemplar... for many things that go beyond sport.

---

[67] Lazily general but true enough for this rock 'n roll scenario.

[68] What a great, deeply interesting phrase that is!

- They've done some daft stuff, too: lost matches out of stubbornness and recklessness.
- Sometimes they've maybe lost sight of the fact that Test Cricket IS different – is more about time than other formats. (That's part of its glory).
- There may be a sense that England, despite thrilling us, have also reduced Tests back towards something *smaller.* Something closer to the boomathons. Brook playing tennis shots against Cummins might be one example of this ungainliness – this disrespect?
- Cobblers. Cricket – all of it – needs to be entertaining!
- Yeh but whaddabout time and that whole slow-build symphony-thing? Aren't we heading towards *everything* being short and crappy? Don't we need something that opposes the consuming brain-death and says "WHOA! Shuddup and listen and watch because this may take five days… and that's part of its wonder?!?"
- *Cue angry, divided silences…*

These kinds of conversations have been live for an age - and I don't just mean the age of the Hundred. It may be disingenuous to draw Baz and Stokesy into the polarized debates about What Next For Cricket, Generally, and whether they bear any personal responsibility for the alleged dumbing-down of the sport. On the contrary, there may be a stronger argument that they really may have saved Test Cricket.

Even here there are buts. Bazball will be used consciously or otherwise as a marker: it's stirred-up opinion. The rip-roaring success; the love and need for dynamism;

the essential truth of that imperative to express – both to entertain and to let the humanity flow. Then also the holes that we can pick around coaching over-simplification, laddish naivety, delusion even.

Stokes and McCullum. 2022/23 and maybe beyond? They shook us up in a good way.

SIXTEEN - WOMEN.

Let's *gush* – do that thing where we don't qualify our ridicu-enthusiasms. That can be fun sometimes.

Quite possibly the most upful thing in the world over the last five years has been the dramatofabulous burgeoning of women's sport. I hope you will have 'your own', but mine are cricket, football, rugby and cycling: yeh, maybe in that order. The continuing boom is *making the world* **better** – irreversibly so, you would think.

It's still (relatively) under-funded, still under-valued and under-supported by the media but sport for women and girls is in a much better place than it was. There are genuine professionals, now, across many activities and whilst role-models aren't everything, that 'ya gotta see it to be it' catchphrase does come to mind. In the UK (and in 'my sport', cricket) there's masses to celebrate, whilst always, always, pushing for more equal dollops of funding, infrastructure, opportunity and respect.

I watch the WSL (pro' football, England) regularly, as part of my everyday blast of sporting enjoyment. The quality of play and of entertainment is very, very high. Finally women are being coached, prepared and supported in a manner that befits their ability and commitment... and that registers the fucking calendar year. 2023/4/wherever.

I reckon about 30-40% of the sport I watch – live or on the tellybox - is female. I *set out* to watch women's cricket, football, rugby.

Across the board there have been improvements... alongside frustrations. Reaffirm: levels of funding, pay, coverage and respect remain significantly lower than for men. Few governing bodies have gotten past the 'financial realities' and into the golden-zone where they decide to lead with what is right. So despite masses of corporate statements on male-female equality (and/or, of course *all aspects* of inclusion) we remain on the slow-moving-pavement towards that aspiration.

That injustice fed into my early interest: when I landed ECB Accreditation in about 2015 it just felt right (and, genuinely, felt like it would be fun) to follow England and Wales Women cricketers more than the blokes.

Mercifully, there were signs that things were changing. The first professional contracts for women had been awarded by the ECB in May 2014, to 18 players. But still this 'historic step' was best described as a kind of token, or certainly entry-level professionalism, and there were still relatively meagre crowds that were (to be blunt) predominantly family and friends. But the vibe was developing; not angrily or quick enough for some of us, but developing. Whenever I could,[69] I would go to the grounds within realistic striking distance; Cardiff,[70] Bristol, Worcester, Taunton.

I remember being at the double-header – an International T20 between England and Australia, in August 2015. (I was sat in the crowd so maybe my accreditation hadn't come through, at this point). The women's game was on first. I felt a bit embarrassed – and yes, angry - at the Universe of Wales for being so bloody disinterested. The crowd was crap... and then fullish for the blokes. But it was a Big Day, for me.

We may, us occasionally-Guardian-reading geezers, aspire to a sort of comfort beyond criticism, on the matter of sexual politics. But quite rightly, we ain't gonna get it. Because we don't deserve it; because we are flawed. On that day I was bloody thrilled to see how brilliantly and threateningly Anya Shrubsole bowled... but this is probably because (like the arse that I am) I *hadn't quite expected* women to be able to do that. Not *like that*.

It was the first time I'd seen women's international cricket **live**. Shrubsole bowled with good pace but the revelation was that she swung the fucking ball miles. It was sensational. It was thrilling. The ball was

---

[69] At this time I was working as a Community Coach, for Cricket Wales. So there was a day job.

[70] A wee note that *may* surprise you: where I live – in Pembs – I am **100 miles** west of Cardiff. Two hours forty-three minutes on the train: drive to Sophia Gardens in a bit less, but not much.

swinging-in so far she could barely control it. From memory Shrubsole got three wickets in the twenty overs, including Meg Lanning, one of the emerging and indeed original superstars of the game. I loved it and have written about it many times – apols, friends, if I'm duplicating. It fired me up.

From then on, my annual planning – hah! – focused more on England Women than England Men, and I have had the real privilege of being in media centres at those particular locations, watching the quiet surge forwards, real-time.

I've seen the transition from Edwards to Knight, and Heather K's own indomitable growth. I've seen Nat Sciver become The One, and Nat Sciver-Brunt. I was there when Amy Jones announced herself (to me, at least), at Worcester, with rich, committed ball-striking,[71] and when Ellyse Perry answered questions three foot six in front of the original handful of compadres in the Women's Media Posse at Taunton. I was also there in Hove when Mady Villiers took athleticism in the field to another level. It's been wonderful.

Now we have a World Game at an authentic international mark. It's true that Australia are utterly boss, and that together with England and India they form the sole meaningful power-block but women all over are fully professional and some are rewarded accordingly. I find it anthropologically and/or sociologically fascinating that

---

[71] Typically, AJ made twenty or thirty, not big numbers. But she hit hard – compellingly so.

our friends Down Under – whom I'm guessing many of us don't have down as Leaders of (any) Enlightenment? – have led the way on equality for female cricketers. Emphatically so.

As per everywhere else, it was a long time coming. But after Commonwealth Bank subsidised Aussie women for the first time in 1988/9 – pretty fundamental expenses, you understand – something clicked somewhere. Players went from taking annual leave from work to play in tournaments or series around the globe to receiving parity – well, almost – with the national heroes of the men's game.

In 2013, major pay rises kicked-in, together with tour payments and marketing bonuses. Then, maaaybee with one eye on developments in Blighty(?), 2017 brought a 'memorandum of understanding' that included women in there with the fellas on the revenue-sharing model. The kitty for Australian Women's professional cricket bolted from $7.5 million to $55.2 million. Arguably better than that, it was agreed that all players in both squads should receive the same base-rate remuneration. Soon it followed that the prize money for both the (male) Big Bash League and the (female) WBBL would be equal. And guess what? Australia's Women have battered the opposition ever since.[72]

(This situation has been evolving quickly: there are plusses and minuses, inevitably, with the Big

---

[72] O-kaaay. Simplification. But Australia being better-resourced and supported than everyone else has surely played a part.

Three – Eng/Aus/Ind – still being the only nations realistically able to find Big Money at this stage, and the international governing body showing a predictable lack of inclination to spread the dosh around. So hard to be *up to date*. But Women's Cricket is **HERE** because of the explosion in opportunity, inspiration and quality driven by authorities catching-up on what is right, in terms of policy and resources. There is small-print: like the disparity in retainers paid to women and men - even in Australia - but this is overwhelmingly a Good News Story).

*

After that Shrubsole Moment I applied for and received accreditation for every England Women's international I could get to. This meant conquering my impostor syndrome and slipping quietly in to media centres/press boxes as though I was some kind of legitimate member of the corps: initially tapping away on my i-pad, cos it was marginally more reliable than my clapped-out laptop.

At that stage TV and radio coverage was less sumptuous and there would be the same five or six people doing the Written Press thing. (*Notes to universe*: this really hasn't changed much. The women's internationals I attended in 2023 still only attracted about six, maybe ten writers of whatever sort. An equivalent male game would, I promise you, attract between 30 and 50, depending upon the import of the fixture).

So yes, whilst things are better, the fact of the sexist universe still presents itself to us. There *will be* five times as many journo's attending Eng v Aus or India Men than there would be for the women's contest. Most of the media does not and would not attend a women's match; mostly (or partly) because their editors ain't gonna send them.

But there are significant plusses. Alison Mitchell, Ebony-Rainford-Brent, Isa Guha, Mel Jones, Melinda Farrell, Adam Collins and Dan Norcross (amongst others) have all 'taken off' on the back of radio and TV coverage of female cricket. They deserve it. They have been there from the beginning of meaningful media and have earned the right to be the voices and faces of this game.

Mostly, as the token clownish bloggist on the scene I keep a relatively low profile. Only some of those named above will have a clue who I am, despite us nearly rubbing shoulders over a period of years, and none of the players could put a name to my police mugshot. (This isn't quite modesty: I just do my thing and don't bother with Pressers[73]). I'm not anti-social, I hope – would never fail to acknowledge a friendly smile or comment - but you don't always get that, from the wider press pack. Fair enough. These people are busy and some of them are legitimately high-profile. I'm not.

Dan – he of the 'do not adjust your set' shirt supply - was notably welcoming and interested from day one and I have huge respect for Adam's work-rate,

[73] Press Conferences. Generally rehearsed platitudes – male or female. Boring.

professionalism and long-term backing for women's cricket. It's genuinely gratifying to see them become real worldies of the media gang. They are both authentic supporters; some – of course – aren't.

(It's not a competition fer chrissakes but I should probably be noting another coupla folks here, for their commitment to the Gunns and Knights and Scivers and Brunts of this world: and I am happy to do so. Stand up, Syd and Raf! Let me also tip my metaphorical hat to a) the general idea that women are hosting, widely, now and b) the likes of Alex Hartley and Kate Cross, who seem fabulous and have already contributed generously and entertainingly to the wider media).

I do attend men's internationals and Finals Days. It's there that I have gotten to know George Dobell medium-well. Outstanding writer and good, good man. His support of Azeem Rafiq has been smack-on, courageous and bloody important.

It would be intrusive and indiscreet to say too much more about 'How it is – the Press-box!' So I won't. I *don't go* for the camaraderie, in this instance. I go because it's a real privilege to have the access and the facilities and the people looking after you. Whenever possible I grab the finest of fine views – straight down the strip - and great nosh and endless coffee and water tends to come with the territory. But mainly I go because the cricket and *the vibe around it* has got better and better; as I/we knew it would.

(Vibe? What vibe?)

I mean the play; the crowd; the feel of it. The quality of the action and the senses bouncing or bubbling-up around the ground. The hitting, the bowling, the fielding, the athleticism. Danni Wyatt. Nat Sciver. Heather Knight pouring her cool oils. I mean experiencing something really good... as it gets better.

*

What have I seen, then, to make me feel so sure that this is good? That *you should watch*, if you ain't, already? Masses of things. Surely it's raging obvious that the standard is high, now, and that you/us cynical old blokes can finally pipe the fuck down? Room for improvement, yes, but scope for celebration and dancing round the living room? Too bloody right mate. Which brings me to Australia. *First.*

This is not to suggest I'm non-tribal.[74] But they are the best and they are worth that, arguably, for those groundbreaking moral/political shifts: Cricket Australia dun gud – at least on that. Their women are the best-paid sportswomen Oz have, and probably the highest profile. Australia Women dropped the Southern Stars moniker in 2017, because their blokes didn't have a nickname, and because, maybe, it just sounded a bit meh. Better equipped and better prepared, they swiftly took the game to previously unthinkable heights... and then on again.

We're into new territory, with regard to *exposure*; most of it good, some of it edgy. Ellyse Perry has been what

---

[74] HA!

the media would have rather blithely described (until about 2000-and-something?) as a 'poster-girl for the sport'. But plainly and rightly, we're into a kind of post-glamour era. We need more intelligent ways to describe and discuss the roles/force/profiles of (sports)women who are now bursting through into levels of fame that simply didn't exist just a few years ago.

These are matters of sexual politics which I am simply not well-placed to get into. What I will say, because I have second-hand-but-personal experience of the dangers of body-consciousness and image, amongst young females, is that the demon 'socials', in this exploding universe of intrusion, criticism and scrutiny, may work concerningly against any new generation of stars. Being the 'face of' this or that, however skilfully presented by club, country, or the media, could be a dark challenge.

Perry is just a tremendous natural athlete who has carried herself with extraordinarily unassuming grace, given her generational talent, through times of relative innocence, into the Instapresent. She continues, supremely *and* quietly, somehow, to make this all about the sport. Towards the end of a glittering and truly inspirational career, she is still diving around to make boundary stops that would hospitalise most of us. I have loved watching Perry field - never mind the other stuff.

Elsewhere for Australia I've liked Megan Schutt's inswinger and her bunny-hop-shuffle: her skilled, persistent threat. Also Lanning's undemonstrative imperiousness; Mooney's quiet belligerence; Ash Gardner and Alyssa Healy's god-given, dynamic brilliance. Bladdy great, mate.

For England? The whole charging-after-Oz epoch has been a ride in itself. Within that, the baton passing from Edwards to Knight and the latter's muted but stout-hearted leadership has made for a fascinating tale. Knight has been down a long road, long in a good way, more perhaps in the way of a stalwart than a star. Amateur then Stormer or Hurricane.[75] Strong on that deep-running stoicism-thing. But developing: now you see stiff uppers, now you see sixes bludgeoned straight. Un-showy, old-school quality: a Proper England Captain. Seeing Heather Knight be both the rock and the Unlikely Mistress of Occasional Boom has been a real pleasure.

Maybe Knight's one for the regulars. If you have just gotten into this then firstly – welcome! Secondly, go watch Capsey, Wong, Filer, Bell, Kemp; some of the relatively New Kids. But look out for Wyatt's fielding and batting; Mady Villiers *throwing;* Sophie Ecclestone's lovely, individual but world-leading twirl - and the certainty of wickets. And Tammy Beaumont's finch-like twitch and swish. It's fun.

I will be there, I hope, maybe inevitably comparing the new England stars to their recent forbears. Like Brunt K – as was. Steaming (in or mad), generally, but an absolute worldie. Bowling stonking away-swingers

---

[75] Western Storm, Hobart Hurricanes; amongst others.

or absurdly cute slower-ones across that divide from 'no-one cares' to packed stadia. And now her wife, Nat, still finding it all too easy: at another level, the only issue being about whether this lights her up enough. (Keep going, Scivs; it lights *us* up!) England Women. Still chasing Oz: still with work to do. Worth a watch.

*

Down the food-chain a little I've done some coaching of women and girls. In schools the majority of the cricket and P.E. I've led has been mixed but outside, on pathways, it's been separate. When I started off there were virtually no female coaches. Now they are still in a significant minority (in my experience) but of course it's wonderful and important that they are there. I am ver-ry clear that it's preferable for young women and girls to be led by female coaches: I look to stand down if I am in any way blocking that.

It's a particular kind of privilege to lead people who identify differently[76] and in my own flawed way I try to respect that. And fail. I'm too old and too loose and effusive with my language and manner to avoid errors of sensitivity – but believe me, I am trying. Probably trying harder to be better now, than ever before: and yes this is bound to be partly because expectations, quite rightly, are much higher.

---

[76] Ver-ry nearly wrote 'members of the opposite sex', here. Which would illustrate *all kindsof points*...

For some years I've been coaching and volunteering at a particular club; hilariously, I'm now playing, too. Hugely conflicted about naming the club and the individuals so will defer on that for now. But after leading All Stars and Dynamos (junior training) sessions, for years I was asked to support a potential women's team. I hesitated – or thought about it – to allow space for either a younger coach or ideally a female leader of whatever sort to appear. When it became obvious that they really did need a voice, I stepped in.

Fast-forward to NOW, two years on, with a whole club transformed. Why? Well...

- The women are absolutely loving their (softball) cricket!
- There's a strong cohort of women involved – not just in the playing, but that was the *way in*.
- (I have pretty much stepped away because) confidence and understanding of the game has soared, so that training and practice has been managed from within the group.
- Already it is clear that family members are 'tagging along' and joining in, either with practice or with tasks around the club.
- These women are great, generous, committed people. They pay subs; they help with juniors; they get on the committee. They are proper *keen*.
- Women are leading this, now. They are turning up to train and enjoying it. They are winning games. The universe of our club is richer, deeper, better.

This, if anything, is an under-appreciation of how brilliant this has all been. And I know (from kinda being in the trade) that this sort of *development* is happening all over.

*

Further, brief, shameless celebration. Or symbol, maybe?

Within the last fortnight Alex Hartley has been appointed spin coach to one of the male cricket franchises in the upcoming PSL - Pakistan Super League. Hartley has just retired as a slow left-arm bowler for England and various short-format club outfits. She has swiftly become an outstanding addition to the media-sphere, where she offers both professional insights and that hard to pin-down experience - *great company*. Now she will work for Multan Sultans (I kid you not) as a specialist spin coach *alongside* Cath Dalton, the former Ireland fast bowler, who also has a coaching gig at the franchise.

These are firsts... and therefore Big Deals. I can only hope the two women get the respect and attention they deserve from the clutch of international stars they will be coaching.

SEVENTEEN - HONOURABLE MENTIONS.

At this stage of the writing of this book – October 2023 – something happened that confirmed my inclination to drop in a few more thoughts on inspiration, a word I'm reticent to use. The truly great Bobby Charlton died. If we were on-line here I'd probably say bugger all else but link to the three goals for England in World Cup, '66, all of which speak to his brilliance as a shifter and striker of a football. Job done.

The absolute screamer against Mexico, that flies across the keeper into the top left corner as Charlton saw it, is unarguably an iconic moment in English football history. That gathering (almost fifty yards out) and recognition of the space in front. That shimmy before easing right for the shot. But then the drama goes *beyond* those movements, into the rich dreamland that is sport-as-something-else-entirely. And in doing so, despite the drag of generations of clichés[77] - some of which will inevitably repeat on these inadequate pages - it *affects us*.

---

[77] I say this, whilst also thinking that the clichés have *a role to play* in the memory of these things. Maybe that's why we can't shake them off? (As well as – yaknow – the lazy writing!)

Yes, the technique is grooved over a zillion man-hours. And the import, the occasion makes it stupendous. But does any of that de-mystifying stuff *actually de-mystify it?* No. This finds some extra dimension as mind-blowingly as it found that far corner. How? How can it be *both* bang-to-rights obvious that we're seeing something purely physical *and* yet we just inadvertently grabbed hold of granny's arm? Because it's so thrilling and so rare and so vividly dramatic that it feels somehow heavenly – like we're in the presence of a god. Charlton's gleeful, instinctive, beautiful strike is godlike.

We talk about a sharp intake of breath at moments like this: we may even experience it – I still do. I could write a thousand words or more about Bobby Charlton's patent humility and decency, and how that makes him special, too, but this is what I think we should and will remember. The guy was a player; a wonderful, wonderful *player*. And he struck the ball as cleanly as anyone who has ever played at the top level – so presumably as well as anybody who has *ever lived*. *That goal* was definitively iconic. Watch the footage. God-like.

*

We could fall into talking about Charlton's comrades, here; Duncan Edwards, George Best, Dennis Law, maybe? They all drew a breath or two, amongst us on-looking mortals. Edwards was before my time but I saw Charlton, Best and Law play once or twice, live. I was a young kid. The floodlights were on. It was magic. I realise now that this was a particular privilege.

They were extraordinarily different characters and talents who brought a kind of colour and brilliance and sometimes mischief into our lives. Three disparate idols you could not take your eyes off. Does it mean anything that I think of only the one of them as a celebrity?

*

Scoot forward. The Women's Euros. 2022. England's Lionesses win the bloody thing – the first major trophy for Ingerland since '66. And it's the wimmin.[78]

Number One: this is brilliant, on about fifty-seven levels. Number Two: a memory. Related – and related to Charlton, perhaps?

We're at the following World Cup. England have been mixed but done the Southgateian skulk[79] – I know, under Sarina Wiegman! - through the group stages. (By this I mean they've been unconvincing and played relatively little fluent, confident football. But gotten through).

Nigeria in the quarters. The mildly absent James stirs foolishly to get herself sent off and we go to pens. Crunch-time. Chloe Kelly has the opportunity to win it. Shrunken by the moment? Nervy and pallid? Nope - she absolutely dances in and smashes the ball! She pings it

---

[78] Not indulging the irony. Was it just me amongst ancient blokes wot got weird(?) vicarious(?) pleasure from the Lionesses 'getting in there, first? Or *next?*'

[79] Tad ungenerous... but you know whaddamean?

like some willowy banshee. It's the most extravagant and wonderful strike; childlike, glorious, defiant, free. This is one of my moments of the World Cup, not because it's Ingerland, not because of the immediate repercussions but because it was utterly, thrillingly emphatically done. *That* was *All The Meaning*, thank you. Often 'statements' are laboured and thin. This was fuck-ing fabulous.

*

Let's extend this meander a little. Again, expect no conclusions as such, but I'm hoping that the constellations of memories and ideas that flood out will coalesce around certain understandings or values. If I say that I want, just briefly, to get into Dutch football then that makes me think that we're moving on with our particular themes.

Clough, Guardiola, Silva, Best. Foden. Cruyff, Krol, Neeskens, Bergkamp, Seedorf. We can argue about whether there's a pattern here but not, I think, over the common link to the primacy of skill. And maybe intelligence? But in what sense, if any, is that or was that intelligence shared? Is it describable or should we leave well alone? We're dealing with abstracts as much as we're dealing with *systems,* yes?

I haven't, frankly, had the time or inclination to go look for signs that Mr Clough was inspired by or inspired the marvellously watchable Dutch teams that illuminated world football in the mid-late seventies, when Clough was at or approaching his own peak. It seems natural that both parties would be aware of and hopefully respectful for the others' achievements.

The Netherlands, under Rinus Michels in '74 and Ernst Happel at the '78 World Cup, did that thing where they played the best football – Total Football, as it became known – and were overwhelmingly the neutral footie-connoisseur's favourite, but somehow contrived not to win the grand prize. (In my dotage I may go watch every available game they played between about 1970 and 1980 and see if they were done-in by lack of physical presence, average playing-surfaces, or what? The lack of a Jules Rimet for Cruyff and Krol remains one of the great injustices in the history of the universe).[80]

If Clough's teams were playing now, they really might look quite like City. Passing and shifting. On pitches that make it possible for skill to dominate. Ditto the Ajax sides that were instrumental in bypassing opponents rather than bludgeoning them or being better physical or athletic specimens.

Forest and Derby were a tad more prosaic than the teams stacked with Oranje Gods but the aspirations towards slick movement and comfort on the ball were there. I do wonder how much better these teams (in particular) might have been on the modern billiard tables, with greater protection from referees. Anybody who ever attended the Baseball Ground in about 1972 and takes those memories to any top-flight football club

---

[80] Do I exaggerate? Barely.

now, will re-calibrate their respect for the players of that era of mud and sand... and smile – wryly.

Surfaces would be better at international level but the impish lads we called Holland had not the slicked, immaculate surfaces that Frenkie de Jong and Nathan Aké take for granted. But my god they could play! From this suddenly extraordinary distance – 45 years, give or take – it feels like Krol, Mühren and of course Cruyff could be transplanted with consummate, indeed spell-binding ease into the Guardiolasphere. If only.

*

But we can't and don't want to just talk about football. Our personal Pantheon of Wonder & Respect would have to include references to Welsh rugby, to the Baabaas and to the British (and Irish) Lions.

I was very much a young English lad when the mighty Edwards and JPR were lung-burstingly and fearlessly projecting themselves and their ecstatic nation into the world's startled consciousness. (Wales? World-beaters? How – just *how*?!?) But, strange as this might sound to neighbours and friends now,[81] I remember back then feeling some *share* in their brilliance. Maybe genius – Barry John, Gerald Davies – really does transcend geography and tribe? Maybe we're simply back to that thrilling quality?

---

[81] Now that I've lived in Wales for forty years, that is...

I've said that my Dad was a rugby man as well as being neck-deep in footie. He certainly both loved and appreciated the great Welsh teams and, maybe crucially, was big into the Lions. This may have given us access, or opened that door more fully: the lads in red - well, both reds - became *ours*, now.

I'm honestly not sure how much any of us think about how we legitimize our sportspeople (in terms of tribe) but there must be some fascinating processes at work. In the case of The Rugby, I can say that I am certain that a ver-ry real connection exists - a very real pride – around the Lions. From Gareth Edwards to Jac Morgan, through decades in which money seems to get increasingly central to the Lions Project, there persists a dreamy, almost mythic quality to the award of caps that soars past any worldly cynicism. Rugby People, players and fans, know that it's an ultimate, for bold lads from Limerick or Westward Ho! to get the call. It's a badge of honour as much as it's a sporting achievement. Levels of respect and sheer effort-into-the-cause are quite remarkable. Even now.

Despite the concerns about the astronomical costs and therefore the inevitable, increasing gentrification of tours, in particular, the Lions are special. Special because of the quality of matches (typically) and because our petty squabbles[82] are rendered irrelevant. Yes we all moan like hell that Our Lot are suspiciously under-represented in the squads, but come game-time we go

---

[82] Actually significant political/philosophical differences, which I absolutely acknowledge.

apeshit in unison. Some of the best watches of my life have been Lions matches, in Welsh pubs. We roar the lads home, no matter where the fekkers are from.

*

The Barbarians is like Lions but with more laughs. (Although this is not to say that there haven't been *episodes*). And the Baabaas are selected with entertainment value as *the primary concern*. They are about pitching wonderfully talented players into a matchday squad of mixed internationals or performers anybody would want to watch, and then telling them to sling the ball around. In addition to the elite-level playing-thing, and the cross-fertilization of national tribes, the Barbarians code is strong on twinkle. And it is *invitational*, opening-up that space to provide fabulous, improvised theatre.

Having *just this second* watched Alun Wyn Jones – just the 158 caps for Wales - wax lyrical about precisely this, describing it as a "special thing and a huge honour", I'm going to close this out. The Barbarians are much-loved, again by players and fans. They get the rich connections and the rich import of this daft idea that mischief, risk, flair and skill are important and somehow transcending. Lads & girls – there's been a Women's Barbarians since 2017[83] - await the call like we used to crowd around the radio for FA Cup draws.

---

[83] Sadly, no Women's Lions just yet – though allegedly preparations are underway.

"You're in!" being a pulse-stirring equivalent to "Liverpool, at home".

*

Every sport has its gods. Or 'gods'. Just *what is it*, about them?

I'm both fascinated and also spend half my time actively re-coiling from any strategic un-picking... cos they're just wunnerful, eh? Let it be. Clearly they fulfil the need for profile, money, entertainment, adoration. Less clear is the mechanics of genius and the merits or otherwise of fame. And I'm not sure if time makes any of this less enigmatic. So their indescribable sportswonder is in this book – and you choose the names, when we meet down the pub!

It's fun to make those lists but easy to get caught up either in the Cult of Now, or wearing those fabled rose-tinted specs. Hierarchy, chronology and value are not phenomena we can easily sift. There may have been an innocent era which enabled a purer breed of hero but even in the time of image rights and flamethrower walk-ons sport can and does deliver drama that cuts through the bullshit. But something loometh.

The brutal truth of this is that though we've had significant numbers of truly great women in sport, we're massively less likely to experience the wondrous heft of their achievements... because they're women. The level of exposure and respect and remuneration for them has typically been waaaay down on their male equivalents.

(Without over-thinking), Star Women for me might mean Korbut, Billie-Jean King, Comaneci, Graf. Then from Our Lot the likes of Denise Lewis, Ennis-Hill and Nicole Cooke[84]... and then some cricketers or WSL footballers. (Tomorrow's choice would be different, depending on profile and particular triggers). Throw that question at my twenty-one year-old daughter and she returns sharply with Victoria Pendleton and Simone Biles, but admits this is partly because of stories outside of sport.

Our Blokey Universe had Higgins and O'Sullivan; Piggott and Dettori; Bradman and Botham and many, many more. They all felt MASSIVE. Though as we have said there's still a powerful imbalance, in terms of male/ female presences, it's changing a little. This is good. Roll on the next lot. May they identify in different ways.

---

[84] A rather good example of a Forgotten Worldie? A) Woman. B) Cyclist – and therefore 'lower profile?' Cooke deserves her own chapter, in here, but yaknow, space and time (and tbf, have written about her before).

EIGHTEEN - RIGHT NOW.

Hmm. Checking, over my morning hot lemon. *Things* wafting in; you know how it is. Like the minor concern that a few readers will be wondering if this flowery stuff on genius and inspiration is supposed to be in some way *comprehensive* – to be completely representative. The polite answer is "no. Don't be daft". And also "yes. Well, maybe *indicative*"...

I have chosen not to dig out all my faves, or all the ones I can remember: most of them would have been Local Heroes, and therefore unknown, but possibly still recognizable, to your good selves. (I was tempted; tempted even to write a list of the names, so as to mark them into history, admittedly rather niche history, in a quirky book that maybe smallish numbers will read). Haven't done it. Followed the hierarchy-of-instincts, instead.

Arsène Wenger should patently be getting a look-in, with all this talk about culture and skill. A ludicrous omission, particularly as he was in many ways the trailblazer towards what we might even call multicultural football, in terms of style and origins. Feel also perhaps I should have left Guardiola a little more exposed to criticism, or maybe re-calibrated him against Klopp more fully. And should possibly have added in the clear memory of the six-week period in which the splenetic Tüchel rode his hysterical wave at Chelsea marginally more brilliantly than either Pep or Klopp could manage – and all three sides were ahead of anything else in the football universe. (Yes! Am clear that briefly, Chelsea were the best footballing team on the planet, with City and 'Pool close behind, during a moment of extraordinary, ravishing quality). But I've covered that now.

Not *regretting* the Guardiola inclusion, but let's insert a sentence here, about how Klopp is almost certainly a richer, broader, more lovable human, who has captured something truly special about his club and found a way to convert that (through his own magnetism and heart, as much as through football knowledge?) into irresistibly urgent teams. Does his inclusive, soft-left man-hugger vibe not feel closer to us than Guardiola's dense, strategic ecstasy? I think so.

Liverpool are more directly intoxicating than City: arguably, more exhilarating. Klopp's budget for team-building has been significantly less than that available at the Etihad. There are times when, like all of them, he is out of line on the touchlines... but I like the man and I respect his talent. He feels real.

*

Here's something weird and wonderful. Age does not or need not reduce your appetite *or necessarily your capacity* to wallow in sport. (And by wallow I mean *actually play*, as well as revel in). We all probably know walking footballers, or ageing tennis-players, or the oldies down at the bowls club. But we may be less aware of the grinning but frequently pot-bellied groundswell that is Seniors' Sport at large. 'Vets' or 'age-group participants'. Like me. There are shedloads of us, hangerloads, some walking stiffly out, in our fusty kit or snazzy coloured clobber, raising a hand to the dazzling sunlight like strangely agreeable zombies.

This is both me... and not. It's both mainly male... and not. Or *won't be*: this, too will change – will be another universal improvement.

I started playing cricket regularly last year after a break of more than thirty years. Ridicu-fact: I bought my first pair of cricket spikes, aged sixty-one. Could be my particular frenzy of denial but I've not yet – not quite – capitulated to the shuffle in and bowl spin tendency. I try to run. True, sometimes I'm patched-up with compression bandages, (something I'd never heard of until about three weeks last Wednesday) but yup, this deluded soul's been measuring-out sixteen fullish yards for a 'run-up'[85] and going dangerously beyond a jog.

I am no longer, if I ever was, an exceptional athlete, but I am throwing myself around (and into the bowling) more than most of the guys who have crossed the

---

[85] Prob-ably now reduced to 12, because of yaknow – niggles.

boundary into Senior-dom. (Let's call it Seniority?) Why am I still launching? A) Because I can't stop and b) because bowling a cricket ball has always been just the fabbest thing. Especially when you try to bowl as *quickly* and as well as you can. It's both one of the great, whole-body sporting movements and a kind of lush finger-painting. I am going to be bereft when I can't bowl.

Cricket has been a huge part of my life, for aeons, but barely credibly, I have not been playing – stuff got in the way. Now I can indulge and it's completely wonderful. I play club cricket on a Saturday and Seniors whenever possible – generally Sundays or midweek, evenings. Love both, but the latter is an absolute revelation in terms of the comradeship, sportsmanship, quality of play and sheer enjoyment. (I knew it would be, meaning it surely can't be a *revelation*... but it's such a love-fest of so-o many treats we can bend the rules, eh?)

Overarchingly lovely is the idea that the number of daft old buggers staying in or returning to the game is **growing** exponentially. The Pembrokeshire Seniors Posse – over 50s/over 60s – has more than doubled, in eighteen months. Most of these guys have been or still are good players. For some, this is important: the competitive edge may not be attractive or necessary to all of us – get that – but it does play an invigorating or essential part, for some. I am delighted to confirm that though games are healthily animated, all are genuinely welcome and (mostly) opportunities are shared. (This of course may get trickier as numbers and therefore standards rise. It's likely we will put more than one team out).

Since you ask, standard-wise, I fall into my own category, having barely played league cricket, but catching up via some knowledge, decent coordination and the aforementioned reckless keenness. The buzz around this is seductive and yeh, motivational. We're all out to prove stuff I suppose but if it goes tits-up we're probably gonna laugh. The craic is exceptional so word has gotten around that *something's happening*. I can confirm, friends that it really is.

*

We're moving towards a section about Sports Development, in which we may try to shuffle our foaming idylls into strategy, or the discussion thereof. Having worked (effectively) in that sector for more than a decade I do hope to be able to throw a little expertise into the mix. But an entry-level observation might be that the growth we are witnessing, *across multiple Senior activities,* is a tremendous positive. These individuals – you, me – are having the most wonderful time whilst (of course) simultaneously giving their whole bloody lives a joy vaccine. Physical health – boom. Mental wellbeing – boom.

In the matrix of umpteen health crises (and crises of provision) this is profoundly good. Society needs fit, well people: we can't afford the alternative. *Enjoyment* is such a key part of activity. Diet and activity levels are key to wellbeing. Pembrokeshire Seniors are here because they made me, a relative outsider, so welcome and because they reminded me how special the hwyl[86] around teams can be. It was nearly too late: but I know I'm not the only one feeling that new lease of life.

To my knowledge, most senior sports are funding-free or certainly funding-lite. We're a freebie for the local Sports Development crews. It's striking in Pembs that just a few fellas have put a few things in place – independently - and then palpable pleasure has done the rest. (Oh, o-kaaay, with a little help from WhatsApp and the Twitters).[87] We've got this thing going by talking to our community, the cricketmob: about how much of a laugh it's been.

---

[86] Welsh. Spirit or craic.

[87] Yeh, I know. X. And all the worse for it.

PART THREE: THE CASE FOR SPORT.

NINETEEN - TEAM/ COMMUNITY/TRIBALISM.

The sharp-eyed amongst you may have noticed that principally we've been banging on about teams. I have been known to stand in front of a new class or group of players and tell them that this word - teeeeeam – is my favourite, before going on to a) press the fun button and b) sort some activity in pairs or groups, or 'whole-class challenges'.

This is only partly daft energizing. The rest of it is nailed-on truth. Team pretty much *is* my favourite word – or at least I think it's a concept loaded with power and opportunity and scope for improving the universe. (A-and for those with concerns about the competitive essence of team sport, I say I hear you. And hope you've understood the unspoken stuff(?) in here, about filling up the soul, not the trophy cabinet? Competition is not normally an evil... but of course it needs to be appropriate).

Anything approached intelligently is going to draw conflicts, yes? So my consideration of the value of teams can and should both gush *and* acknowledge the dangers of particular kinds of adversarial practice. I try to cover this baby early-doors, when I'm coaching young cricketers. We talk about what's ahead and what my hopes and expectations are. In that first meeting I will be saying that more than anything, I'll want all of us to work towards becoming a *gang of mates* who look after each other. And I will probably mean it.

None of this gregarious guff means I don't like golf or fishing or chess or yomping solo on the cliff path. I do. Plainly solo pursuits can be every bit as rewarding and stimulating to the heart and the soul. But honestly? I think maybe I've been at my happiest when larking about with a bunch of other people: players. That feels like an unconflicted truth.

*

I'm not sure if that happiness has been contingent upon the standard of play so much as the standard of company, although this is another blurred 'insight'. I was probably record-breakingly happy to steer a ridiculous drive with the outside of my left foot[88] into the faaar top corner from an obscene angle and range, for Poly FC, in about 1984. But it was no more fun and certainly drew less communal delight than the diving catch which removed the leftie superannuate batting at no 10 for Wales's Really Quite Oldies, in September 2023. In fact the shockwaves and the craic resulting from the latter may have been as fabulous and funny as anything in my sporting life. Jesus we laughed: "that had gone past you, mun!"

Teams *are* wonderful. For their bringing-out-the-brilliance-ness; for their lols; for their capacity to genuinely raise-up,

---

[88] Right-footed, see?

or support. But having grown up through the notorious 1970s, a period when football violence was so scary and so rife, it would be plain disingenuous to omit some discussion of the godawful negatives around our tribes. Sadly, the hatred between certain groups of fans has barely dissipated: football is safer than it was back then but there are still some wild men about.

Sociologists and psychologists are much better placed than my good self to describe the causes and the processes acting upon these individuals (or 'firms') but whether the fires burn from geographical tropes or largely through some hellish, excluded disenchantment may be irrelevant to those on the receiving end.[89] Folks are still getting battered, or worse – but less often. Alcohol-bans and CCTV may both be unfortunate but they have been effective, in and around grounds. I have been shit-scared going to football: I hate that fear and the shame that hangs around and isolates the game in this respect.

Trying to account for the violence by contextualizing or reaching out into wider issues is both an important and civilizing instinct: however, in the face or presence of booze or cocaine-fueled 'aggro' the overwhelming sense is of sadness that we are so evil and so weak. Fans at war. Did you ever hear of anything more pathetic?

---

[89] Merill J Melnick's 'The Mythology of Football Hooliganism (March 1986) cited *eight myths* about perceived violence &/or perpetrators, whilst noting a 72% increase in cases of personal violence between 1974-84. (Home Office figures). The Daily Telegraph of 16th May 1986 is quoted as saying 'since 1979, youth unemployment has doubled while youth wages have dropped considerably'.

But there are buts. Tribe can be wonderful. Most of us will have been somewhere where it seemed natural and even essential to sing our hearts out to support something or someone of ours. Most of us are proud of our immediate clan, or our regional group, or our nation. The pull around these things is extraordinary and often thrilling: positive.

I left my hometown forty years ago but on every trip back, always timed for a home game, have been genuinely moved by the sight of grown-up men and women (and often their kids or grand-kids) streaming in towards Blundell Park. In their black and white shirts; along the bleakish main drag; or down the greyish, terraced streets. Otherwise-normal people, joking or acknowledging Jonno from down the road, or those same faces queueing for a programme then for a slash. Daft and poignant and quietly stirring. There *is* magic here.

I can't pretend to be Grimsby anymore... but I do... and I am. And I am weirdly proud of my Primary School comrades, now turned middle-aged supporters, who *really do* anchor their lives around that yomp, that bellow, that roar. "Maaaa-rrrii-neeerss!!!"[90]

*

---

[90] GTFC supporters have another chant which simply repeats the line/question/fact/invocation "All Town aren't we?" I love that this is a call to loyalty and place, but somehow transferable to every place. Because even in our myopia we do know that every club (in every sport) has fans who feel exactly this: that this is home.

My life and work in sport may be all about pushing the notion that Orn'ary Peeps can become something ver-ry different, once over the white lines. How many guys or gals do you know that launch themselves as personalities and as talents *only* when they get on a fucking pitch? I know hundreds. Sport isn't the only thing that develops folks but christ almighty it does develop folks. And maybe the real, (counter-intuitive?) alchemy is that this has nothing to do with the level of performance.

Coaches are in the business of facilitating: 'orrible corporate-sounding word but it's what we do. Enable folks, as individuals and as part of a team. I'm *really fascinated* in things which may apply across the diaspora of standard(s): which are about the human more than the event, perhaps. Surely team humour – the nature, the hwyl, the spirit, the level of togetherness – is a BIG FACTOR in team success, *however you may judge* that success?

I've mainly worked 'in the community' – another phrase that might mean nothing, but I take it to mean in schools and clubs. (Am guessing the cricket pathway work I do kinda crosses over into a specialism, of sorts). Anyway, I've not been responsible for that many Olympic golds, or on many silverware-hoisting coach processions, or been shit-faced at Number 10. But I do know about being in teams, in tribes, in communities pulling towards something. Not sure I finished up working in Sport Development *because* of this cornball altruism, but I hope my experience and knowledge of squads and games and wins and losses *and value* has fed in to the coaching and teaching I've done.

But what we in the trade call 'delivery' is but one small part of Sport Development. And the next chunk of this book will be about some of the other stuff. Preparing for and administrating the 'interventions'. 'Insights'. Strategy. The processes around and behind what gets offered to communities.

I'll be trying pretty hard, as per, to avoid this getting too dry – believe me I probably could write manuals on coaching or community strategies but will continue to battle against that. Too dull. I will be trying to make the upcoming toe-dippage feel relevant, interesting, colourful, even. It's all that and more: Sport Development is where all of our wider concerns about sedentary lives, mental health, wellbeing find their focus. It's also the place where jarringly disparate issues (like how the hell we pay for the NHS and why kids think there's nowhere to play) have to cosy-up. We have to find a way to make activity central. On.

TWENTY - JUST ONE EXPERIENCE.

An indulgence if I may. But one which fits. The following is a blog from 2015, when I was proud to be a Community Cricket Coach for Cricket Wales/Chance to Shine. I nearly re-titled it or sub-titled it 'Placing Teddies' but no: it's unchanged from the original. Copied and pasted from the website; for the craic, and as a way in to our section on Sport Development.

An indiscreet note: I didn't want anyone to be traceable as a result of this. But feels like I can add (now, at this distance) that the 'boy I'm not going to describe or name' was in fact a girl. And in case you're wondering, *I* am @cricketmanwales – or was.

Just One Experience – bowlingatvincent

Disclaimer: certain things have been changed here so (I believe) no-one could be undermined by the following story. I'd like to think that wider interests – much wider than me or mine or Cricket Wales's – might, can and arguably should be served by recounting what follows. It's healthy, it's heart-warming and it really happened.

Right now we're test-driving a project that (rather than gathering children and 'migrating' them into local cricket clubs) is offering them an indoor knockabout. The kids get @cricketmanwales, his partner-in-crime C****, a hall, some kit and then we play stuff. Once a week, for a few weeks: out of school hours.

I don't want to get bogged down with the whys and tactical wotnots but (because two of you may be interested) we're doing this for the following reasons, amongst others:

- The Leisure Centres are available to us now.
- Local cricket clubs don't have the capacity for us Cricket Wales peeps to drive yet another clutch of budding Under Nines or Elevens into their hands – or at least they're telling us they can't accommodate a new team – fair enough.
- Some kids just don't or won't feel comfortable in the club environment – maybe they aren't 'good enough' (or don't think they are) to make anybody's team? Maybe they're a wee bit scared that they'll have to face a Proper Hard Cricket Ball? Maybe Mum or Dad says it'll cost too much?
- Simply, we wanted to offer a different opportunity and, without actually targeting any particular group, without remotely abandoning the idea that clubs are rightly at the centre of what cricket is, see what a mildly alternative space and opportunity might offer.

This may have the sound of a *fringe* project, an experiment and there's some truth in that view of it.

A little. But though I confess to indulging in occasional meetings about this strategic stuff, rest assured, dear friends, that we are *about* the cricket – the act, the action that happens when a daft bugger like me is let loose with a bunch of kids. These weeny earthlings don't feel a part of any project. They're too busy moving, catching, stopping, starting.

We've called the sessions 'cricket hubs'. We didn't, on the poster that my daughter ultimately cobbled together, specify 'beginners' or anything else other than 'Boys and Girls, 6-11'. I then did some sessions in local schools and Bigged the Thing Up in an assembly or two and then off wee went… we knew not where.

At the Leisure Centre, as a familiar face to the arriving children, I 'lead'; which is a posh way of saying it's me that does most of the shouting. Given these young 'uns do turn out to be anywhere from six to eleven years old and do have a fairly alarming but fascinating range of abilities, the sessions have to live off my sense of what they can do – what they can have fun with – and maybe what's possible to learn.

At one centre a boy I'm not going to describe or name joined us. When I say joined us, he slid in with what felt like an unremarkable degree of reticence. After a welcome to all I ran a warm-up game. Amongst the giggly anarchy I saw that maybe we needed to place a few balls – asitappens, we were using anything from teddies to beach balls to foam rugby balls – into his hands rather than either let or expect fellow players to lob things at him. He was involved on the periphery, neither happy nor unhappy but with his hands unconvincingly outstretched, at the risk of either failing to acquit himself or being by-passed by 'better players'.

Don't panic. This post isn't going to be about the quality of my coaching. It's about the quality of this wee lad's experience. Sure, I'll take a modicum of credit for getting fairly early on that he wasn't, in the dangerously contentious phrase, a 'natural'; that the games were going to have to come to meet him. I reckon I also probably intuited something about the appropriate level of fuss he'd most effectively 'respond to' and just quietly kindof revisited him, now and then, to show tiddly things, without focusing on this fella as the Possible Struggler in the group.

Interestingly – and unusually – the boy's dozen compadres were mostly children who clearly found catching and coordinating movements generally a challenge. Maybe this helped. We played some simple games – yup, including that ole chestnut hitting from tees! – which everyone could do and I hiked the technical info with certain individuals when they need to extend. It went okay.

This went on once a week for four weeks. The boy attended every week and to my knowledge did not speak a single word to either myself or one of the other children – even when asking for a pass, a catch. He simply got marginally more proficient, more convincing, at the body language, the shape of the movements, in proffering those arms. In time he tried throwing, bowling, all of it; they all did. Skills, in between or in and around what we might call small-sided games.

He managed, found a way through, without either busting the proverbial gut, or getting frustrated, or making spectacular leaps forward. He was it seemed in that undemonstrative middle-ground.

The fifth week comes and the boy arrives a tad late. His mum (whom I've seen, watching discreetly but never met or spoken to) does that 'would you mind if I had a quiet word?' gesture and we step out of the hall momentarily. She says something very close to this;

Look I just wanted to say thank you, really. I don't know if you know but my son has some really significant confidence issues – really significant.

I say I had an inkling but...

No they're really debilitating. And I just wanted to thank you because he's NEVER EVER done anything like this. He just can't. So he never does anything.

I say something crass like 'that's genuinely lovely to hear, thankyou'.

No, thank YOU, it's remarkable – are you going to be able to keep on going with his? He got up this morning and asked what day it was and when I said xxxxday he said 'Oh great – cricket tonight!' Believe me he NEVER says anything like that! So thank you.

People, I was more than a bit choked. I managed to blurt out something about the cricket going on again after Christmas and then went back in to join C***** and the kids.

On the How-Rewarding-Was-All-That?-o-meter this ranks pretty high. Maybe because it felt both literally (eek!) awesome and a little mysterious. How could this lad's seemingly non-animated encounter with our cricket-thing turn out so... profoundly? I'm delighted but also shocked, almost, that he's found it so enjoyable – frankly it didn't really seem that he was having that much fun. Whatever that unknowable process, we find ourselves reflecting on a stunning example of the fab-you-luss-ness of... what? Games? Movement? Interaction? Those few encouraging words?

Good to reflect, for one minute. Because I'm thinking this is evidence of the power of sport. This young boy has now bounded more than slid – albeit in his own, magical, ghostly-silent way – into a new expanding universe. He is both denying six years of absence and disengagement and bulleting towards possibilities previously unthinkable. Why? Because he enjoyed the movement, the encouragement, the sporting challenge. It acted as a trigger.

We may never understand quite why this worked. It may not matter. But the fact of it matters. The quality of this boy's experience was such that things were transformed.

That I suppose is anecdotal evidence. We can't 'map' it or prove it so as to legitimize ourselves in the eyes of local authorities or funders. It's pretty much non-measurable. But know what? To me it feels like a really great bit of work.

TWENTY-ONE - WORK EXPERIENCE.

Okay so what have I done - I mean to get me and that child to that place? What were the processes acting on the three parties; her, me, and the host developer, Cricket Wales/Chance to Shine? Some of those questions I will answer. But why does it matter?

- 'Just One Experience' is not fiction: it may sound kinda crass to some of you but I think it's a decent example (these get called 'case studies', right?) of potentially profound development through activity.
- Soon after our sessions, the girl 'who never does anything' joined a local sports club.
- It's mind-blowingly obvious to many of us who work in sport or who are neck-deep in games that they can become a gateway to a zillion wonderful things but some of you don't get this; don't buy it or understand it. You are wrong and we need to convince you.
- In a universe where budgets are being cut, and where the authorities generally vastly under-rate the possibilities Physical Education/activity for wellbeing can offer, I am going to advocate bloody hard, for Sport Development. Because we need it higher up the list of priorities.

- The fact is that surveys of young people do show worrying trends towards unhappiness, lack of physical confidence (and therefore personal autonomy) and sedentary behaviours.
- (Consequently), I will back up my enthusiasm-frenzy with significant piles of independent evidence. Because this is plainly necessary, for this diversion into the nuts and bolts of the Case for Sport to hold any weight.
- Oh – *and because I was recently employed by my Local Authority to revisit and make sense of a whole series of national reports on activity and wellbeing.* I will share sources where possible, and para-phrase some of the **key insights,** where professional courtesies feel appropriate.

I may need to start with this: how did I get to the insights role? What happened before that which legitimizes me as any kind of worthwhile 'voice' – on anything? Simply for brevity, more bullet-points:

- Born into a football family. Grandfather a pro', Dad close to that level and an outstanding athlete. Mother likewise; hockey and tennis – Hong Kong Ladies Tennis Champion! Brothers who live for sport.
- *Endless hours* of outdoor activity, growing-up; from obstacle-courses to building dens to climbing trees to playing togger ferabout eight hours *every day*. Goodish at football, cricket – ball-games generally. Played regional football and basketball as a junior. Captained adult football teams.
- Did entry-level football coaching certificate. (May not have completed). Became volunteer cricket coach

and underwent ECB Coach Education – loved it, weirdly! Attained Level Two then completed the six workshops leading to Level Three (but younger, better coaches placed on the qualification course by my County Board). No issues.

- Became Community Cricket Coach for Pembrokeshire in 2012 (I think). Attended multiple 'pure cricket' workshops over a decade or so, under the likes of John Derrick, Matthew Maynard and later Mathew Mott, at Glamorgan CC and elsewhere. Joined Pembrokeshire then Cricket Wales West Regional Pathways as a coach.

- Underwent continual and diverse training for Cricket Wales/Chance to Shine. Everything from ethics to efficacy – on both the strategic and delivery side. Cricket Wales were early adopters of specialist training around Sport Development. Enjoyed working and learning alongside Create Development and other providers. (Ridicutruth: coaching and teaching sportstuff is waaaay more sophisticated than most of you would imagine, now).

- Have led training for fellow coaches or aspiring coaches, on ECB Projects such as All Stars and Dynamos.

- Latterly I was also employed by Sport Pembrokeshire as Peripatetic P.E. Staff. Underwent further training in Sport Development, notably under the #RealPE Programme. ('Cutting-edge' holistic practice; ver-ry strong around the idea of providing inclusive pathways[91]).

---

[91] A key issue for P.E. is that still there are too many kids not getting hooked. Often these are disaffected and/or disadvantaged

- Was also employed by Sport Pembs to oversee and offer an account of the Happen Survey – an enquiry into mental and physical health amongst schoolchildren. This work was extended and broadened so that I could report on a whole raft of contemporary enquiries into issues around activity and wellbeing... and draw insights. These were then factored-in to Sport Pembrokeshire's wider strategy.

This is why I'm feeling entitled to rattle on about a) sport (or *activity*) and b) what we might do with it. This, obviously, is no academic treatise because that's not my territory. I *did,* however plough through a pile of surveys that would probably be familiar to every Sports Development lead in England and Wales, and I went at it with an appropriate level of professional diligence. (I just didn't write it up in academic or corporate language: that was the whole point). Given the financial climate and the increasing imperative towards making good choices, our mob felt we needed to *really look* at what's needed most... and what works in terms of delivery.

---

individuals. Their drift from engagement, generally, and physical confidence specifically, is a MASSIVE SOCIETAL ISSUE.

TWENTY-TWO -
THE CASE FOR ACTIVITY
(NOT JUST FOR SPORT).

I think it's very likely that the overwhelming majority of the population, if asked, would advocate for more activity; in schools, in the community, at home. Indoors and out. We all get that activity is good and probably that it is *necessary*. Some, like me, might argue that though we'd rather make our case around enjoyment (and therefore mental as well as physical health), it's critical to accept that the Money People are likely to be relatively immune to our calls to enthusiasm and experience.

Money People – those who have money and decide about money – may be blind to the obvious. (Yeh – o-kaaay, or have 'wider remits'). This does not mean we capitulate to their one-dimensionality. We make our arguments better, and whilst fitting them to their limited worldview, we also call out the mad myopia, diplomatically or otherwise.

It's madness to rundown or underfund almost any kind of activity. It's madness that Physical Education remains un-expanded and un-recognized as a central part of school life. In the era of suicidal introversion and murderous peer-pressure, it's madness that kids aren't being offered movement that fits with their needs – that they may not even associate activity with pleasure. We've let the bar fall drastically.

We have to wade into both politics and philosophy, here. Governments both national and local are culpable, and so, of course are we. All of us should be bawling about unhappiness and sedentariness in a similar way to calling out poverty and racism.[92] I'm raging angry that the current Westminster government[93] is shamelessly taking us backwards on all these issues – deliberately so, on the latter two – but they are not alone in averting their eyes from the international crises around wellbeing.

Governments have *never* acted remotely proportionately, or proactively upon health. They are not doing it now. Set aside the criminal selling-off of the NHS. Governments have been told for decades that too many people are unwell or physically illiterate – that is, unable to express (and be stimulated positively, by expressing themselves) in a physical way. We are reaching a low-point NOW, because issues within and without(?) our control have massed, and we are walking into a crazy, self-inflicted slow-motion ambush.

---

[92] Ah. Contentious, agreed, but I just mean this is MASSIVE. There is no hierarchy, as such.

[93] Have to put a date on this, for obvious reasons. Tories; 2023.

- T'internet. We all know everything and our kids are being twisted by most of it. They have to have such-and-such and have to look like her or him.
- So in a universe of obsessives... and 'quick-fixes', why would we care about activity?
- Bankers can have their bonuses but 'there is no money available' for education. Or health. And the Arts? Don't be ridiculous. Good luck with anything that smacks of abstract notions like the lifting of the soul.
- Families *do get* quite good information from schools, but in the deluge of advertising around junk food (and in the absence of good cultures or money) people older and younger are getting fat, unwell and less able and/or inclined to move.
- Zoom out and there is no moral compass, no understanding much less recognition of what is immediately urgent, for our fellow citizens. There is no drive towards health and happiness. For all the talk and the schemes, The Authorities are not driven by that.
- Besides, the earth is dying so, yaknow, what's the point?

These are some of the arguments for capitulation, yes? I don't accept them. I oppose them and I hope you will join me, hopefully in a more articulate and effective way. But I do oppose them and however feeble it may sound this book is part of that opposition. So let's get back to making the case for sport.

*

It's *economically vital* that we get more people fitter – in every way. The NHS can't sustain this many folks with diabetes, with weight issues, with depression, with poor movement. Maybe set aside blame, here, but accept that if we look at causes[94] – and we *have to*, right? – some level of personal responsibility is in there with the governmental/educational/cultural negligence. Would that be fair?

It's a cruel truth that in the same way that some folks are equipped to deal with and thrive under capitalism, some are less confident or competent regarding movement. In bundling ourselves forward towards stuff *that's palpably better*, let's be generous (rather than judgemental?) towards those who find themselves exposed.

Twiddle the dial, a little. It's *right* that we aim to get more people moving. They deserve it, we need it. If we understand the benefits (and the joys, fer chrissakes!) of activity, then it's incumbent upon us to share that bonus around, bankerless though it may be. The world gets better when we do this. There's a philosophical and arguably a spiritual aspect to this... and all of us – yup, *all of us* – have some understanding of that.

All of us felt good, moving somewhere, somehow. Felt the pace or the grace of it. Or watched and maybe

---

[94] I'm dabbling, appallingly, towards causes, because *whole other book*, etc. But plainly nothing changes without investigation and understanding...

twitched a little. Was it music that set us off? Or the encouragement of a friend; a teacher; a coach?

I seriously contend that every human responds or is drawn to movement at some level. It's in us. Why else would them kids in Pembroke Dock start giggling and then *launch themselves so freely* and with such excitement, when some daft old bloke suggests 'high knees' or the 'smiliest skip ever-ever?' It's in us and we need to find it: sharpish. Not only are we knackered and sad as individuals without it, that weird, faint, unattainable thing 'society' is wounded, critically undermined.

*

Sport Development is the political and administrative wing of Physical Literacy, in the sense that it's the department (of your Local Authority, usually) responsible for nudging us towards confidence and competence in our movement skills. However fundamental they might be. We can be gloriously expressive or concerningly un-able in this regard. Some will actively want the bite of competition; others will be shy of or disinclined towards that mark. The fabulous, frightening challenge for those in the hierarchy of our Sport Development Posses, as I learned over the last year or so, is to have both the philosophical will and the resources to cater across the range of 'would be excellent' to 'scared, unable or disinclined to even start'.

Having been in that strategic mix (as it were) I can tell you that tough choices lie ahead. Nobody in Sports Development wants to wind anything down, not when

Our Patch is screaming at us to widen and bump up the offers. You have to start looking at what you can justify the most. And what works, not necessarily in terms of ticking boxes, but certainly with reference to what draws funding. *Even when you know* that **everything works**, everything has a value, whether it be Just One revelatory Experience that shifts a life, or the tiddly incremental shuffle towards a minor community goal. Every activity counts. But not every activity is going to continue as we are.

This is why I will be both raging and trying to compose some sort of compelling argument in black and white. On this paper. Something that hauls *me* back towards the rational and sticks *your nose* into issues we all sense, but maybe lack unequivocal information upon.

Everyone like me who has seen and experienced not just the transforming brilliance of sport but the transforming brilliance of sports coaching is bound to feel this stuff is obvious. That because we see some wee human light up nearly every time we step out onto a pitch or court or playground it follows that everybody knows: that everybody's as sure as we are that movement can and does transport all of us to another place. But humans of all ages and inclinations don't necessarily know this. They haven't had that moment.

This section in this book is partly the direct result of me getting more real about this. So what do we do?

- Persuade people.
- Walk in their shoes.

- Get really good information.
- Walk in their shoes.
- *Really look* at/listen to what they are saying.
- Work out what's achievable, in the light of all the information you have – and, probably, all the resources you haven't.

Let's look at some surveys before we try to suggest how we might turn our causes into strategy.

TWENTY-THREE -
OUR SURVEY SAID.

Feels wise to come over all practical. So nuts and bolts, firstly of a Sport Development Department and then of the Happen Survey, as an example of a survey tool and a brief description of the how-this-works side of things.

Your Local Authority will of course be responsible for the education in your (state) schools. Every few years the names of the various departments or Areas of Learning in schools will change, as will the curricula. Certain subjects (guess which?) are Core Subjects: Physical Education is not one of them, despite being expanded thematically, so as to reach more directly into Health and Wellbeing. You may not be surprised to hear that I believe strongly that the artist formerly known as P.E. is cruelly undervalued and should certainly be a Core Subject, with that significantly broadened role.

Typically, Primary Schools will not have specialist P.E. teachers on their staff, whilst Secondary Schools will. Local Education Authorities will have Sport Development teams who can provide staff who then deliver activities: these are often called something like Active Young People Officers. Levels of funding available will determine whether the LEA can provide these for free, or whether schools will have to pay for either the AYP Officers or folks like me, who were or are Peripatetic PE Staff.

My experience suggests ver-ry strongly that the good people in Sport Development in the various roles, from deliverers of PE to Disability Specialists, Community Engagement staff or administrative officers, are exactly that. Good people. Plus well-trained, professional and extraordinarily committed. We love sport. We also get that many kids don't... or lack confidence... and that a huge chunk of our work may be around building very fundamental skills, or that essential ease within the active environment. (Like I said; the teaching of sport is now tremendously informed and highly-skilled). Sport Development is being cut.

*

Happen – Health and Attainment of Pupils in a Primary Education Network – or the *Happen Survey*, was designed by experts from the Child Health and Wellbeing Department of Aberystwyth University, based around questions from the Children's Society's Good Childhood Index. I delivered it, into schools in Pembrokeshire in 2022.

This survey was Wales-wide, anonymized and contained 58 questions, with sections under Physical Health and Mental Health and Wellbeing. Subdivisions included Motivation to be Active; Diet and Dental Health; Sedentary Behaviour and Sleep; Concentration; Physical Competence; Physical Activity and Active Travel.

(You will note that this was not just an enquiry into 'sportiness'). Schools received their own brief but worthwhile report, showing their 'scores', against national averages, upon completion.

I confess that despite my growing understanding of the legitimacy of the non-delivery side of our department, I went into this fearing that the whole malarkey might be something of a tick-box exercise, with limited value and without that foundational ingredient (for us sportspeeps), recourse to personal experiences of *actual sport*. I am now better-informed. This survey was cuter, more skilful and more sophisticated than I expected it to be. (I should also note that most authorities ran the survey *alongside* delivery, partly to measure efficacy. We did not).

Though I remain clear that the value of activity is not always best expressed via *this kind* of exercise – pun intended – it's plainly the case that smart, unthreatening, balanced questions can and should be asked, of whichever 'target population'. (May I also note at this point that it was only through getting deeply familiar with this survey that I recognized that a manic enthusiast like myself, wearing shorts and sleekish black sports-clobber, looking medium-hunky and tanned,[95] might not be best placed to deliver any such enquiry. Any subtle or subconscious suggestions from Yours Truly, even when trying to be non-interventionist, would be unhelpful. And unnecessary; because Happen was smart).

---

[95] Insert cheesy grin emoji – obvs.

One minute on methodology, here, before we move on to results and implications. Certain schools accepted the minor interruption into their time and let Yours Truly into their computer rooms (or similar), in order to run the on-line survey. I made clear it 'wasn't any kind of test' and that children could opt-out at any time. Class groups; so typically 20-30. Most questions were of the multiple-choice variety, inviting children to mark against statements or levels of motivation they identify with. It was made clear that stress was banned; i.e. being unsure was fine, the general truth was perfectly adequate, if it didn't seem possible to be certain. Also, that this was **completely private**: any personal questions could be answered without fear of exposure.

In this way the surveys felt entirely unthreatening and, for most children, mildly interesting, I think. The Happen Survey took between 20-30 minutes for participants – aged between 7 and 13 – to complete.

I'm going to offer a few questions, from the survey – para-phrased, to avoid any copyright issues - but accurate enough to give a sense of the nature of the enquiry.

Did you eat breakfast yesterday? Yes - At Home/Yes - At School/No.

How did you travel to school YESTERDAY? On the bus/On a bike/In the car/taxi/Walked/Ran/jogged/ Scooter/Skateboarded/Rollerbladed.

What did you do for MOST of your break-times YESTERDAY? (This includes lunchtime).

Sat around inside or outside/Ran around/Stood around/ Walked around.

How many friends did you play with?/I like to play on my own/1-2/3-4/5 or more.

I think you can see already that Happen is broad... and searching-in-a-good-way? More questions:

In the last 7 days, how many days did you do sports or exercise for at least 1 hour in total? 0 days/1-2 days/ 3-4 days/5-6 days/7 days.

In the last 7 days, how many days did you watch TV/play online games/use internet etc. for 2 or more hours a day (in total)?/0 days/1-2 days/3-4 days/5-6 days/7 days.

In the last 7 days, how many days did you drink at least one fizzy drink?/0 days/1-2 days/3-4 days/5-6 days/ 7 days.

In the last 7 days, how many days did you eat take away or 'fast foods?/0 days/1-2 days/3-4 days/5-6 days/ 7 days.

Reminder: we used this information in a Sports Development Department.[96] Just a few more: these *were* on activity. Children had to select one answer

---

[96] You get that I think this is great, yes – the recognition that lifestyle is health, and absolutely the business of sportspeeps?

from the four choices – strongly agree/agree/disagree/ strongly disagree:

I want to take part in physical activity

I feel confident to take part in lots of different physical activities

I am good at lots of different physical activities

I understand why taking part in physical activity is good for me

What motivates you the most to take part in physical activity and sport?

I am driven by enjoyment

I am driven by having fun with my friends

I am driven by learning and improving my skills

I am driven by competing against myself

I am driven by playing and competing in a team

There were more, key questions on happiness around school, location and family. But for me it's already clear that if we extrapolate out to the full 58 questions, and then to the 8,823 participants who completed the Happen Survey in Wales, in 2019-20,[97] we have a whole lot of interesting and important information about how children see themselves. This material is

---

[97] This number came to hand. Similar numbers over the last several years.

being factored-in to decisions on which games your kids play in their school. Quite rightly.

*

For me, amongst the really big-hitters emerging from this survey was the fact that in almost all cases children were *motivated to take part in activity by having fun with friends.* In many groups this scored at 100%, compared to lower percentages (always) for playing competitively and/or in a team. Friends first, even above 'enjoyment', results-wise... because friends *mean enjoyment*, yes? It was also fascinatingly clear that very high percentages of children know and understand that activity is massively important, and yet do not or cannot find a way to act on that knowledge. We will speak more on this.

*

I wrote those last few sentences on the morning of Wednesday 8th November 2023. The *day before*, Mr Dan Roan had posted a story for BBC Sport (and News) about changes underfoot at Sport England. That giant governing body had hoiked its priorities around towards disadvantaged communities and/or individuals: the story reported £250 million specifically aimed at inactive, deprived groups. This followed the trialling of 'Local Delivery Pilots' in 12 selected areas. The Beeb quoted research that:

'A quarter of adults in England are currently deemed to be inactive, with more than 11 million doing less than 30 minutes of activity in total a week'.

It went on to include the recommendation from the House of Lords Sport and Recreation Committee 'that responsibility for sports policy should move from the Department for Digital, Culture, Media and Sport, with a new minister for sport, health and wellbeing as part of a "radical" shake-up of sports policy'. The committee also said Physical Education should become a core national curriculum subject in schools, and called for a new statutory requirement for local councils to provide and maintain facilities for physical activity.

Does this make me think that the tide is turning? I'm afraid not – not particularly. For political reasons, largely. But at least the import of the challenge to get us all fitter is landing in some powerful corridors.

I expect to see more of the shift towards prioritising disadvantaged groups. Generally, pinched funding may sharpen up the choices, for better or worse. It certainly makes it more important for developers to demonstrate change and improvement. But is *that* always good? Prioritising disengaged groups feels an increasingly obvious option, in the context of budget reduction, increasing social division and wildly variable opportunities. Some might call this change of direction 'levelling up'. The difficulty is which sectors get left behind, post the switch?

*

I personally delivered the Happen Survey into local schools and spent a lump of time trying to understand what the nationwide results, over some years, provided to us by our colleagues, *meant*. But I then went onto delve medium-deep into several other relevant surveys, including the Good Childhood Report, from The Children's Society. (We'd agreed I should do this because a) there was funding and b) frankly, nobody previously had ever had the time to do anything beyond a quick skim of the conclusions. Despite understanding the value and integrity of these documents).

The Good Childhood sources are seen as significant because the surveys have been running for over a decade. Therefore meaningful comparisons can be made. Material of this sort is naturally complex and sometimes contradictory: my brain *really did* hurt trying to un-pick workable truths or clear pathways towards sound, justifiable strategy. Let me offer two examples.

Firstly, the concerning but not entirely unexpected revelation that the latest survey (unaffected by Covid) showed a significant decline in children's happiness within four of the six areas examined: life as a whole; friends; appearance; school, compared to when the reporting began.

Secondly the finding that Good Childhood reports over time have consistently shown that the vast majority of children score *above the midpoint* for all six measures of happiness. Which begs the question what does the midpoint of happiness mean... or represent... or feel like? (I'm being slightly facetious but my point is that even if 'scores' are clear it may be hard to quantify what an acceptable or healthy level of contentment might be). However, this finding *is* important perspective: just not at all to be used as a barricade against necessary, radical action.

*

I'm conscious that this could be endless. So let's round-off by underlining that as well as studying the Happen and Good Childhood Reports, I looked at relevant material from Sport Wales, our own in-house Pembrokeshire School Sports Survey, Child Poverty in Pembrokeshire and the Levelling the Playing Field report from Senedd – the Welsh Parliament. All this in order to draw insights we could use to improve the quality and impact of our own Sport Development work.

I wrote two reports – one specific to the Happen Survey and the other to account for the wider investigations. If this was Match of the Day, think of the following as the highlights.

No particular order... and I may not refer back to all of these... so take me at my word that these were *amongst the most important insights*. Please read carefully.

• **The intervention session is only the tip of the iceberg, the visible tangible part.**

   Building relationships and showing you care are the critical element. Making pupils feel welcome, confident and valued is essential

- it is notable (as a general point) that the longer children are in school, the less they feel 'their ideas are treated seriously'.
- Recommendations: pupil voice and choice should be respected, as far as possible. Relationships with school KEY. Make the interventions relevant.
- Despite quantitative data being easier to present and compare, anecdotal evidence, case studies and informal interview seem to capture impact and progress more effectively.
- School and appearance are the domains where more children (aged 10 to 15) have reported being unhappy across 10 years of the Understanding Society survey.
- 'Various studies suggest there is a disparity between current available provision for physical activity and *what Young People say they want*. Current opportunities are often seen as *too traditional*, *overly structured*, and *not enjoyable*.'
- Children are motivated towards activity most strongly by *'having fun with friends'*.

Inscribe all of this on my gravestone.

TWENTY-FOUR - HOW?

The 'key learnings' that conclude the previous chapter are robbed straight from the brainstorming document I put together for our Sport Development Posse. As I turn now, towards *making the idylls into strategy* the concern again breaks through that some of you good people will be thinking about nipping down the shops, or aimlessly swinging a golf club, or *anything*. Bear with, briefly. This will not be a manual. And even if you do view it as niche... it's important-niche.

The universe is screaming that we must be active – for our mental and physical health. That's not remotely contentious; therefore we must act. Personally, I put the urgency level on this as high as acting against climate change: and the Case for Sport has less flat-out refuseniks! Nobody denies the crises around health, and only the worst kind of 'politician' will 'fail to recognise' the moral or economic imperatives in play.

I quite like the admittedly dangerous argument that we all have a civic duty to look after ourselves but completely accept there are MASSIVE BUTS in terms of our individual abilities and capacities to follow healthy lifestyles. Authorities of whatever sort can't be draconian about this – economic and cultural factors are acutely deterministic - but it's also true that *it would be good* if we all aspired to *do more*, literally and/or metaphorically.

The job of the teacher or coach, volunteer or paid, is to work hard and well towards spreading the inclination to be active. I've said I think it's in there, and stand by that. Babies move to music, pre-birth. Little kids giggle and run, or bounce, or flap, before any self-consciousness kicks in. We must be active, so we practitioners must keep that instinct going.

It really is key to grab children early. And not let go. But sadly the failure of governments/society/authority/ education/that miserable headteacher to recognize the transforming grace/economic import of Physical Education puts an early block on mass comfort (let alone joy) in liberating, individual movement. Sure, the crushing forces of a sedentary homelife, available gadgets and the sense, justifiable or otherwise, that 'there are no safe places to play out there', are all conspiring against us. But there is stuff we can do.

Political-level change has to be the starting point; money and respect for the primacy, not tangentiality of *lifelong* activity. Meaning investment and provision. Cut the cloth somewhere else: pour resources towards the somehow ludicrously 'indulgent' idea of healthy, happy people. A monumental culture-shift: but get on it.

In practical terms this probably means targeting the kids: most for us (society) to gain, there, and for them it's not too late, not if we light them up at 5, 6, 7. But from early-doors, we need to be *listening*, too, and stretching as far as possible to provide them with things that they and their friends *enjoy*. This means great, individualized, sensitive delivery but alongside a transformative widening of the PE offer, thinking outside of the traditional repertoire. If the kids want cycling/trampolining/yoga/horse-riding/basketball/surfing *try and make it happen*. Or at least make it known that you are a) listening and b) trying to change things up.

All the reports converge around the idea that despite a zillion words being written or raised regarding Pupil Voice, kids don't feel like we're listening, not just in Sport Development - in *schools*. Worse still, the heart-breaking truth is that the longer children are in school, the more they feel they are not being listened to.[98] This ain't just teenage angst. It's a systemic failure. So yes of course there are 'realities' crowding-in; and 'limitations'. But we do this better and we start with Pupil Voice.

*

I've said that delivery of sports is now light years ahead of the ancient, wildly inappropriate traditions for slinging groups out on muddy pitches and whistling at them aggressively. (It bloody *should* be better than this, and largely it is). That other soundbite 'holistic health' has bitten deeply in to those former travesties, so that P.E. and Sport Development staff are bringing richer, cuter sessions than was previously the case. But children

---

[98] There in black and white, in the surveys. Trust me.

need to be doing more[99]... across a wider spectrum of opportunity.

My research did lead into some dark places. Findings from one particular cohort of local students were so concerning I can't share them here. Disaffection with school and life was distressingly evident. And trends around this estrangement or disillusion appear to persist.

This from the Good Childhood Report:

Young people with lower life satisfaction scores at age 14 were more likely to have negative scores on mental health indicators at age 17 than other children, and to say they had self-harmed in the last year, or ever tried to end their life.

The bigger picture itself is concerning, particularly as many of our assumptions about links between health and poverty are so strongly confirmed. I wrote this across my notes for one of our brainstorming sessions:

*BIG-PICTURE stuff, but... if **in every reported case** disadvantaged children seem less likely to enjoy/ participate in activity... ARE THERE BETTER QUESTIONS TO BE ASKED? (Even if this is 'beyond our remit', should we not seek to involve ourselves/ influence these discussions?)*

---

[99] Yes. Specifically more hours for P.E./Wellbeing. Appalling and inexcusable that we as a society have allowed this to reduce.

What I meant was given that everything in the research material pointed towards a kind of *ongoing failure* to lift deprived kids towards something positive – everything's relative, but it *does* suggest that - should we not be questioning everything we do, as a Sport Development mob?

Were we trying to cover lots of bases – rightly, but inadequately? Did this mean we had to 'shrink our ambitions', or campaign *somehow* for more funding? As you might expect, these matters were above my pay-grade, but they are at the crux of what most sports providers are now facing. Reduced budgets, increased or flat-lining inactivity in certain communities. These are killer issues.

WHY, exactly (if this is discoverable?) do disadvantaged children report 'negatively?' Why do only about 20% of kids develop a life-long culture of activity?

Above, more questions from my notes. And below, more… with one or two possible answers. Will leave the 'how else?' hanging, for you, dear friends, to consider.

How do we MAXIMISE our response to that challenge?

- *Work harder at providing what children want.*
- *Note the imperative towards ENJOYMENT WITH FRIENDS.*
- *How else?*

*

I offered my colleagues some suggestions and/or prompts/ professional conversation-starters. Looking at lowish Active Travel[100] scores, even in schools where kids were showing strong understanding of the value of activity,[101] I asked the question could we not, at very little cost, support both more Active Travel and improve the key markers for time spent undertaking meaningful exercise? Primary Schools tend to have environmental groups; parents get messages. Why not promote 'walking trains' or 'cycling trains' where substantial numbers of children get into the habit of exercise, to and from school? (Do-able, I reckon). If children and families were encouraged to 'do the right thing' for ethical/environmental reasons *and* for physical/mental health, and if the comparatively minor support necessary was put in place, might we not have a win-win situation on our hands?

We don't always share great ideas or good practice across departments or regions. This may be partly to do with the wee traces of pride and machismo that often bubble up in sporting circles. But whilst working on the Happen Survey, a few of us across West Wales did pitch in our ideas – rewardingly. We heard of 'traffic light systems' to check in on young children's moods, during sessions:

"How are you, today?" Thumbs up/5 fingers = good, 1 = not too good. Repeat during session; or at start and finish?

---

[100] Simply that: getting to and from school under your own steam. Walk/bike/scoot, etc.

[101] This was often at 90% plus, under Happen. It made me wonder why children got that particular message but not others?

We heard how some staff found that celebrating young children as Super Heroes really boosted the enjoyment and confidence of many:

Jonny could be 'today's Jumping Super-hero'. Sara could be 'today's Catching Hero(ine?)'

We returned repeatedly to this idea that

Yoga (*or something else?*) which significantly supports WELLBEING & AWARENESS learning, through both ACTIVITY & BREATHING could be the change that children needed – particularly if they asked for it!

Some of us were fascinated and a little surprised to hear that in order to *measure* activity, some providers were using entry-level Beep Tests, to gather data.[102] And they reported back that all the children loved it!

Zooming out a little, one Sports Development department described how they had provided Parental Engagement sessions and after-school clubs to draw in families and support less active and/or obese children. They linked-in with local General Practitioners and with other Community Projects so as to skilfully and discreetly cross-refer individuals. They also provided simple activity kit-bags to try and encourage games at home. There are things we can do.

---

[102] Beep tests are often used in performance environments to really push athletes towards high endurance and/or pace. One argument is that this is likely to be inappropriate for individuals lacking in movement skills or confidence.

TWENTY-FIVE - LEGACY.

Don't get me started on the London *Olympics* Legacy; it's more an indictment than a thing. But clearly the essence of Sport Development – indeed of education – is legacy, in the sense that central to any purpose has to be the idea of improvement down the line. I'm not sure how definitively measurable any Olympic 'bounce' or increase in uptake of Sport X is, but clearly the increases in profile and infrastructure *provide opportunities*. Ideally, we welcome this. But we note that should the Olympic Bonanza turn out to have been largely a photo-opportunity, then the argument that pouring millions of pounds into chasing medals is a twisted, nationalistic obscenity becomes increasingly valid.

Possibly-relevant interjection. A visiting colleague - Sports Development; coach - dropped in to some sessions in our community; schools and clubs. She was "really struck" by how poor our facilities are. Based in New Zealand.

Legacy is about great, inspiring coaching. Coaches and teachers who are agile; who understand that there's a massive range of individuals out there, whom they must try to read and respect and entertain. Delivery has to be of a high standard: holistic; appropriate; engaging;

assumption-free. But all this wonderstuff only really works when it works *for society*; when the critical mass of it can swamp the fears or inexperience or poor experience of the public at large. This can only mean a huge culture-shift, to make activity central to learning.

Please don't underestimate how activity can and does educate; *is*, in fact, a *medium* of education and a way to access other Areas of Learning. It can work in the relatively narrow or specific sense of providing unthreatening or downright lovely access to numeracy. Or PE can light up confidences through team-building or working in pairs, or appropriate groups. These things are real: dip into #realPE or one of the other illuminating projects at your local Primary School. The skills are there to transform kids.

So sure, we'll take the medals, many of us really are lifted by that. But give us a HUGE WEDGE. And some time. Invest in us. In the idea that it's right to get children/people/the universe happy. Invest in the bounce towards movement... and ease in the outdoors... and *pleasure*... and less pressure on the NHS. The alternatives are neither right nor sustainable.

*

I get that the necessary political will needs to land before we can change things. (This is depressing, given where we're at). But in the absence of gigantic piles of moolah you can be confident that your Sport Development people and your people in PE and (increasingly) Wellbeing will be chipping away at this.

And typically they will be impressively cognizant of the multifarious and evolving Good Practices. They don't need my advice but I'm going to conclude this wee diversion into the future by dropping in some learnings[103] of mine.

- Whilst we AYP/Peripatetic PE staff need to have **consistently high standards,** maybe we also need to be original/individual? This means having *ideas* – and being able to adapt them.
- PEOPLE ARE COMPLICATED: MAKE NO ASSUMPTIONS. We would be well-advised to be as sensitive and attentive as possible during every moment of every session. We can make a difference.
- The surveys may suggest that Secondary School children *may be* more likely to be sedentary/disaffected/unhappy (& we must always look to support). But this is not a given.
- You may not need to move a mountain (but move a child). LISTEN TO THEM. *They need to be heard: they need to be seen.*
- …And on that Pupil Voice stuff – the fear, maybe, that we can't deliver on what they want. A) Having the conversations and valuing their viewpoints may be as critical as providing the camel-racing Davy Johnson just asked for. Plus B) look below, at the activities requested… maybe they aren't that outlandish?

---

[103] As they say now…

Sport Pembs survey: Sports high in the **'latent demand'** returns – i.e. *heavily requested* by pupils – include:

For girls: swimming/cycling/trampolining/horse-riding/basketball/surfing.

For boys: football/cycling/motor sports/basketball/swimming/running or jogging.

TWENTY-SIX - THREADS.

Latterly, I haven't always shown the evidence for stuff; please forgive. For one thing I didn't want to write a ferkin' manual. But also, there are gert big gaps in Kandinsky and Miro and – blimey! Maybe these scribbles of mine are abstracted constellations that we travel through? Maybe that's what they *are?!?* I just blasted off and then it was *up to you?*

Whatever; trust me, if I wrote somebody said or did something, they **did**.

*

The section titles here are no cosmic accident. 'Formations' because these things formed me, they're the Big Relatable Stories and I'm hoping they will land with a few of you guys, with or without making you cringe. 'Practice' because you got to, and because sometimes the work of others has just been inspirational. 'The Case for Sport' because it's what I do. I'm happy for any threads between to stream out in the wind: one or two may interlink.

The deeply personal stuff in here is legit, I hope, for its potential reach. It genuinely feels less about me than about the period... and all of us. Not sure there was much in the way of Family Therapy in '78/9: *am* sure our 'coping mechanisms' were somewhat obscured by shock and by our particular circumstances - a Northern family with four lads. We wouldn't have gone to 'get help' even if it was out there.

*

Zoom out. And forward. Maybe things have always been about profile but it seems our vanity and the world conspiracy towards plucking advertising revenue has funnelled us somewhere pret-ty twisted. Pay-per-view. Followers. Image rights. Saudi money. Indian money. Add in the everlasting matrix of concerns about race and privilege – absolutely not just in cricket – and you might fear sport was in a dark place. But without being complacent, some things have improved. Women's sport, mutable, unhelpful concept though that might even be, maybe tops that list. So I'm a follower – an imperfect one.

Jazz Joyce; Chloe Kelly; Alessia Russo; Issy Wong. Need to be planted in this book. They have brought and are bringing the sprinkle of stardust, the shuffle to the edge of your seat. They are legitimate, top-end sports-magical. Forget the silverware; enjoy the moments. Joyce racing and twisting like a salmon in the rapids. Or selflessly, heroically hoisting the invaders back. Kelly just being flash: teasing and curling or inventing space and time where there was none. Russo being the attentive, wandering, all-round-striker-par-excellence: then back-heeling that Puskás Award-nominated goal against Sweden! (Go find; go find!) Wong being patently a star – for everything from her athleticism to her look – but one whose story is currently being challenged. Making the story richer.

In Section Two we looked at brilliance; at what I like to call some of the goodly things. The new-age culture of the All Blacks. The imperfect perfectionism of Guardiola. Messrs Kay and Carey, in that other new-age phenomenon The Athletic, wrote compellingly of his genius and his guts. In allegedly the world's best but most physical A-League, at the moment of commitment, with voices screaming in his head about 'over-playing' and the need for less pixies, more power:

'rather than back down, Guardiola doubled-down'.

City played *even fewer* long balls. They drove their rate of possession yet higher – to an unprecedented 66.4%. They twinkled the division to death, winning it with 100 points, dismantling the record books en route. If we can disentangle how Manchester City played from how the club conducted its business, the accolades pile up with the trophies. Era-defining. A kind of apex of the Beautiful Game. Epitomised by the sliding, easing, shifting grace of David Silva and the fabulous killer moves of De Bruyne. Wonder-full.

Foolishly – but because it's fun – I may have dabbled in unscientific associations. (Put that on my grave, too). Maybe I shoulda just cut this down to my section notes?

CLOUGH/GUARDIOLA/SKILL/GENEROSITY/
WINNING IN STYLE

But it would have been less fun, for me. Hope you feel the same – obvs.

I do like the idea that skill should out but given the need for the 57 varieties of Other Sporting Wondertraits – like character, strength, spirit, wit, humour – this is another warm contention that may not stand up to a grilling. I like that Clough, in his uncluttered genius, found a way to express that conviction through six inches of mud. I love the mischief around any comparison whatsoever, young man... with the Egghead Inventor at City. Clough barely did strategy: Guardiola does the ironing to it.

My other wild speculation remains – says he, as if there were just two! – regarding the (ahem) necessity of relentless sideline coaching and stat or structural presentation to our Premier League #legends. Particularly to subs just embarking. Who needs 43 Things To Think About when you're nervous and just about to get called a wanker by 50,000 Scousers? And – really? – wasn't everything covered, during the week? Find that obsessive technochat hollow at best. Suspect it *really is* 38% football machismo and 12% existence-justification, for the 1300 backroom staff. Note again that the All Blacks coaches – 86% international win-rate – said virtually bugger all, on match days.

*

Worldies, idols, call them what we might. 'Important' – and yet not. Fleeting – and yet not. Watchable? Yes. They probably do inspire us: sometimes this is good, sometimes this is bad. The fact that 10 women have been nominated for the Puskás (beautiful goal) Award since 2020 is unarguably good.[104] Maybe it's less helpful (or maybe it's just right?) that none of those women made it into the celebrated top three, in any of those years. Beatriz Zanaretto of Brazil, Sam Kerr of Australia and Linda Caicedo of Colombia are amongst the 2023 nominees.

*

I've said nothing, yet about the expanded and (Word of the Year alert?) *polarised* debate over short-format/franchise cricket as a whole. This is partly because I still work on pathway cricket. And I'm wondering if I should have written more about women, in the cricket section, or elsewhere. Feeble as I am, it's a significant area of interest and of hope, for me.

From the extravaganza that is the Women's Indian Premier League, which will transform profiles and actually make some of the best or most dynamic players proper-wealthy, to the Women's Super League (of English football), which does something similar, a *transformation* has been going on. It's on such a scale and has such significance that any negativity may seem churlish. But the faux 'pazzaz' and god-awful team mottos (in the cricket franchises in particular, male *and*

---

[104] I checked. I counted.

female), which so-o irritate many traditional cricket supporters with their clear message that 'wee get the dumbed-down universe more than wee get sport', raise concerns. They speak so obviously to focus-grouped strategies and account so little for existing fan-bases (and their knowledge) that the departure towards New Families becomes a ver-ry risky exercise – or one made at some cost.

And so to the Hundred...and the future of County Cricket. Generational factors may, I suppose be playing into my lack of enthusiasm for the former. Plus I'm not sure how authentic the invented tribes can be... and as someone who knows how daft-but-wunnerful that real-gang-of-mates thing is, *that* particular newness feels more corporation-inspired than inspired.

As a lifelong sport developer and populist of sorts, I understand the imperative towards New Families/New Audience – that's a necessary part of the uncoupling from elitism and class that cricket desperately needs. But as that motivation felt a direct, possibly even deliberate threat to a) the Vitality Blast and b) (therefore) the very existence of County Cricket *itself*, there are questions.

I note and accept, of course, the testimony of all the women who have been adamant that the Hundred has taken their careers to another level. I simply wonder if all the resources stacked behind the project had been gifted to the Blast and the Kia Super

League[105] (or successor) might we not be in a similar place, with no chasm between supporters and authorities, and the counties in a less exposed position?

My early support for Western Storm dissipated with the Hundred and the dawning of the facsimile-version, Welsh Fire. Despite the arrival of genuine worldies in the male and female franchises, I drifted. (Muggins had traipsed to Hove to see and report on the women, in the earlier incarnation). Have mixed feelings about this. Utterly acknowledge that it's great that some non-cricket people have joined and enjoyed. Admit my suspicions about the *pretext* could be misplaced. Want the game of cricket, which remains a wonderful part of my professional and social life, to open up and thrive.

*

But stars, eh? They probably are 'essential', to light things up. We can't *really* measure that - not even us sophisticates in Sport Development. We can't: even if we wanted to.

What we do have to do (in any case) is think wider and lower. How do we get through to folks who don't get it, The Ones Who Decide On Things (But Don't Get It) and the ones who yaknow, hate cross-country?

---

[105] Blast being Vitality Blast – T20 competition for all 18 County Cricket Clubs. Kia Super League – T20 comp for the six semi-professional teams of the time.

We have to find allies and campaign. We need backing – and yes that does mean money. We build up facilities and we innovate around low-engagement groups. We 'do a Sport England' *plus*, find bundles of £250 million and put them into sport/activity/wellbeing. Then we get our staff together and look again at the hows.

Re-coaching, teaching and Sport Development in schools we say again; thissss…

• **The intervention session is only the tip of the iceberg, the visible tangible part.**

Building relationships and showing you care are the critical element. Making pupils feel welcome, confident and valued is essential.

Because we know, now, that we must draw-in the reluctant ones (in schools and beyond, in fact). We remind ourselves and the universe of the power and importance of Pupil Voice. Of us listening to them and trying like hell to shift in their direction.

Children are **motivated towards activity most strongly by** *'having fun with friends'*.

There's an argument that if we don't do this, we may still finish up with plenty Olympic medals, but we'll be living in a darkening, increasingly polarised place. There's an argument we're *there*.

So bigger pictures, smaller pictures. A last thought, possibly beamed down from a drone, at 4,000 feet.

Children (according to surveys) generally tell the truth, even in surveys. So what to make of this, arising from evidence within the Happen Survey?

- It may be a minor issue (and *may be* outside of our remit) but generally low numbers feel *'they can play in all the places they would like to.'* Given that children say that this is one way their wellbeing can be supported, can we learn more about this... and possibly address it?

Children were strident around the idea that there aren't enough places to play. Now there can be about thirty zillion explanations for this, ranging from lack of realism on their part, to parental disinclination to let them out. But the numbers were striking and strikingly consistent. All over Wales, kids feeling like they can't just go play.[106] Which feels just a little heartbreaking, does it not?

This goes beyond Sport Development... a-and maybe into Planning Departments? Before going back to being about money. But for me it felt like a marker. Under the theme of The Local Area, Happen noted four things that **children said** could improve their wellbeing.

- More spaces to play.
- More local facilities – walkable, appropriate to their needs.
- Cleaner streets, (interestingly).
- Safer roads.

---

[106] Yup; note the fuller import of the additional words 'where they want'. But still.

I did note that this may be out of our remit but asked the question of our department: should we have some representation on, or contact with Planning? (It maaay be that there are brilliant people up there with wide horizons but have they thought about what children want... because it may be what society needs?)

*

As a kid I lived for sport. Hasn't changed much. It grew me and maybe it grows me still. I suppose I just want everyone to share in that, at whatever level fits them. Let the sensitive and unconfident find a way to romp. Park; coast path; yard or Leisure Centre. Pitch or sea or track. Organised or home-made.

As a coach I see no hierarchy or conflict between hoping that skills will out and the fumbling development towards competence or confidence. We need it all. This is human nature: the instinct and the imperative to get moving. So guess what? Somebody has to fund it - back those who have the nous or the influence to help us extend or re-discover this blessing. Urgently.

A pleasingly unverifiable last thought. I'm looking out, right now, at a portable sauna, beside my home beach in West Wales. It's smoking – in a good way. The owner tells me it's been busier than ever, today, despite the approaching dusk and November cool. Folks have been cleansing themselves in one-hour bursts: searing heat then jump in the ocean. This is the first year we've seen this. Let's hope it's an omen.

Milton Keynes UK
Ingram Content Group UK Ltd.
UKHW040215160324
439374UK00004B/249